COMPASSION
EVANGELISM

COMPASSION EVANGELISM

Meeting Human Needs

Thomas G. Nees

Beacon Hill Press of Kansas City
Kansas City, Missouri

Copyright 1996
by Beacon Hill Press of Kansas City

ISBN 083-411-6235

Printed in the
United States of America

Cover Design: Mike Walsh

Cover Illustration: "A Cup in His Name" created by sculptor
                    Scott Stearman of Colorado Springs.

Library of Congress Cataloging-in-Publication Data
Nees, Thomas G., 1937-
    Compassion evangelism : meeting human need / by Thomas G. Nees.
       p.   cm.
    Includes bibliographical references.
    ISBN 0-8341-1623-5 (pbk.)
    1. Caring—Religious aspects—Christianity. 2. Church work with the poor—Church of the Nazarene. 3. City missions. 4. Social gospel. 5. Evangelistic work. I. Title.
    BV4647.S9N44   1996
    261.8'08'827—dc20
                                       96-1630
                                        CIP

10 9 8 7 6 5 4 3 2 1

CONTENTS

INTRODUCTION

Plagued by Despair, Hungry for Hope

More than 20 years ago I was rummaging through the Wesleyana section of the library at Wesley Theological Seminary in Washington, D.C. It's a fine collection of out-of-print and historical books and records of the man whose equestrian statue stands prominently at the seminary's entrance near American University. In a city known for celebrities enshrined on horseback, I often wondered what people thought of John Wesley on his horse. Not many people know that the only statue of a religious figure on public property in Washington is that of Francis Asbury, Wesley's first American appointment. His statue stands on a triangle in the middle of a busy intersection on 16th Street N.W., about halfway between Washington First Church of the Nazarene and the White House. How many people understand the significance for American society of these two preachers on horseback?

After 12 years of traditional pastoral ministry, I was struggling to find something from Wesley to help me figure out a way to minister to the poor of my city. About all I had known until then was John Wesley's sermons on sanctification as referred to in various theology texts. As I walked through the stacks of musty books and dusty periodicals, randomly looking at anything that caught my attention, I happened upon a reprint of a 19th-century book with the simple title *John Wesley, an Apostle to the Poor.* As I thumbed through the pages, I noticed the chapter "John Wesley as a Social Reformer."

Beginning my ministry during the early days of the tumultuous 1960s, I had begun to feel the way Thomas

Merton expressed in the title of one of his books: *Confessions of a Guilty Bystander.* I felt called to some form of ministry to the disinherited of the city I saw every day, and I think I would have followed that call even without finding support within my own faith community. But when I came upon this information, I had all the support and encouragement I needed.

To my surprise I learned that Wesley earned a living selling his publications. The most widely circulated was not his sermons or theological essays, but a manual of health care. He wrote *Primitive Physique* for the poor of his day for whom adequate health care was an unaffordable luxury. It was published more than a dozen times during his lifetime.

I wanted to know the connection between the wide range of socially redemptive programs Wesley introduced and his Holiness theology. Was his theology and practice connected or unrelated—merely coincidental? Were the social reforms he led inspired by his belief in the possibilities of sanctification?

While pursuing that inquiry, I came upon an even more surprising discovery in the archives of the Church of the Nazarene. I was allowed into an unattended room where for days I combed through old minutes of the first District and General Assemblies. I read all the issues of the *Nazarene Messenger* and the early issues of the *Herald of Holiness,* looking for records of Nazarene-sponsored social ministries during the formative period of the church from the turn of the century until the 1920s. Denominational archivist Stan Ingersol has now compiled all this material into a wonderful anthology—*To Rescue the Perishing, to Care for the Dying: Historical Sources and Documents on Compassionate Ministries Drawn from the Inventories of the Nazarene Archives.* It was first made available for the 1985 Compassionate Ministries Conference and is updated as new material is uncovered.

That brought my quest closer to home. I was sure now

that the Wesleyan-Holiness tradition, with its synthesis of salvation and social reform, was not a passing phenomenon of the Wesley-led 18th-century Evangelical Revival. Wesley's example of street preaching of conversion and compassion continued through the 19th century, spawning the Salvation Army and informing political reforms such as the abolitionist cause in antebellum United States.

The Nazarene archives of magazines, newsletters, and other publications and manuscripts preserve the record. Nearly every Nazarene district publication during those times devoted some time and interest to the care of needy people in Nazarene rescue missions and orphanages. Even the General Assemblies considered ideas to support these charitable church-sponsored institutions.

The 20th century began with great optimism about the possibilities of human progress through religious nurture. As it now stands, the century will end with equal pessimism about society's capacity to solve its critical social problems and about the influence of religious movements. The gap between the rich and poor is widening. The cold war is past; but ethnic, religious, and nationalistic conflicts have fueled dozens of smaller wars and driven terrorism in a shrinking world—a global village where no one feels safe.

In a time when answers to the personal, political, and economic challenges of the age are in short supply, those informed by the Wesleyan-Holiness tradition have something to say if they can recover their historic synthesis of church and society. Our times need what Wesley and his followers provided for an earlier age—evangelism and social reform combined in one gospel presentation. Governments may initiate reforms, but most public policy officials understand that unless *people* are reformed, real change for the better is unlikely.

These days cars in Washington speed around confusing traffic circles displaying statues of forgotten celebrities on horseback—good roosting places for pigeons. Few if any of the tour guides pay attention to these statues.

Tourists rush to see the Smithsonian museums and patriotic monuments. But I have *my own* tour of the city. It includes congested neighborhoods—populated by poor people in dilapidated housing, streets lined with unemployed or unemployable adults, and teens who have given up on the idea that an education will lead anywhere. These mean streets are home to homeless men, women, and families. The alleys and vacant buildings provide cover for warring armies of drug dealers.

My tour also includes the statues of John Wesley and Francis Asbury, men who began a social and spiritual revolution in equally dangerous and threatening times. As it wouldn't work for me to mount a horse and charge around Washington imitating Wesley and Asbury as they appear preserved in these old bronze statues, neither can their methods be overlaid and followed exactly today. Bill Sullivan, Church Growth division director for the Church of the Nazarene, who has encouraged and supported Nazarene Compassionate Ministries around the world as well as in the United States and Canada, has written and preached with urgency about the need to take "holiness to the streets." That's where it began and where it must be now.

Inside the church we sometimes talk as if the Wesleyan-Holiness Movement itself is at stake. Something more important than that is at stake—people, neighborhoods, cities, countries, and continents are in peril. The Holiness message of personal and social transformation will not disappear, but it could get lost or buried again. Meanwhile, the world waits for, and I'm convinced will listen to, those who step forward to lead the way to this dual transformation. It's not either/or. Personal piety that retreats or reacts will not do. Social action that does not reform people is equally inadequate.

This book is a collage of sorts—a survey of readings, reflections, conversations, and reports from those who are trying to do now what John Wesley and Phineas F. Bresee, founder of the Church of the Nazarene, did during their lifetimes. The chapters build on and are encouraged by a genuine grassroots movement of people filled with and led by the Spirit into neighborhoods plagued by despair and hungry for hope. Through Nazarene Compassionate Ministries all of us, not just those in the trenches on the front lines, have a way of knowing about, supporting, and getting involved in ministries making a difference for the better.

⇔ PART I ⇔

Recovering the Mission

Compassionate Ministries, or social Christianity, has reemerged in the Church of the Nazarene during the past decade from a complex set of theological, social, and political persuasions. The interplay of Church and society in the 20th century provides the backdrop for a resurgence of ministries to people in need.

The official beginning of Nazarene Compassionate Ministries can be traced to the early 1970s. The Church of the Nazarene established the Hunger and Disaster Offering (now the Nazarene Compassionate Ministries Fund) to provide financial assistance to victims of natural disasters in Haiti and Guatemala. It proved to be much more than an occasional response to natural disasters on mission fields. The fund has continued to attract donations even without the urgency of disasters. In 1984 the World Mission Division established the Compassionate Ministries office to administer the global ministries made possible by these contributions.[1] Since then, Nazarenes have contributed unprecedented resources to meet the temporal needs of economically disadvantaged people, not only in the underdeveloped world but also in the United States, Canada, and other developed nations.

These developments followed a resurgence of interest among conservative, Evangelical Christians, and Nazarenes in particular, in meeting human need.[2] Through the middle decades of the 20th century this branch of the Christian Church in the United States all but gave up its earlier commitment to serve people in need. The prevailing attitude, if not theology, of the time had narrowed the role of the Church to spiritual, nontemporal activities. Social activism was suspect as being the work of liberal Christianity, which, it was charged, had given up on real evangelism. Following World War II, the government's New Deal social programs assumed increasing responsibility for creating cradle-to-the-grave support, including social security and public assistance, commonly known as "welfare." Destitution, it was thought, had become a thing of the past. While conservative Christians may have opposed political liberalism, they were more than willing to leave caring for needy people to the state and to retreat into reactionary Fundamentalism.

A theology of affluence emerged among the second and third generations of those whose parents at the turn of the century were among the "churches of the disinherited," as H. Richard Niebuhr characterized the humble beginnings of most Evangelical groups.[3] Churches that once welcomed and included lower-income people in inner-city missions within a generation claimed their new wealth as evidence of the blessing of God. Poverty was viewed as the consequence of laziness, if not ungodliness. Social Darwinism, the idea of inevitable progress, won the day even among those opposed to biological evolution. There seemed to be no reason for anyone to be poor. While liberal Christianity saw the solution to poverty in government-sponsored social reform, Evangelicals were convinced that the way to personal prosperity and social reform, if needed, was through evangelism.

The split within American Christianity was almost complete by the 1920s. Mainline churches crusaded for government intervention to end poverty, while the conservative, mostly Fundamentalist, churches turned from the social responsibility they once advocated. They claimed that Christian social action diverted attention and resources from the Church's primary evangelistic responsibility. Nowhere was this retrenchment clearer than in the Church of the Nazarene.[4]

Cities, with their promise of prosperity, had attracted millions of rural inhabitants during the war years. However, it soon became clear that, unlike the European immigrants of the previous century, most of these people were not about to capitalize on the American dream. During the Great Depression of the 1920s and 1930s, the "churches of the disinherited" were composed of people similar to the man down on his luck who said, "I'm not poor, just broke." While the Great Depression and dust bowl days destroyed the financial resources of millions of Americans, including those of Evangelical Christians, there always remained a measure of confidence that Yankee ingenuity would eventually solve the nation's economic problems. But Yankee ingenuity was not enough for the increasing millions of poor people in the cities. In the 1950s cultural anthropologist Oscar Lewis began describing a "culture of poverty," a phenomenon that by the 1980s identified a "permanent underclass" for the first time in American society.[5] Clearly, something new was happening. The entrenched poverty of the late 20th century defied "pull yourself up by your bootstraps" solutions that seemed to work a generation or two earlier.

Change began to occur in the 1960s. Urban riots, the antiwar movement, and civil disobedience awakened the nation to surprising and threatening social unrest. The tranquillity of the '50s ended. Inner cities crowded with poor minorities appeared to some Evangelicals as mission fields close to home. Urban ministry emerged as a geographically focused response by a few innovative ministers to the ghettos full of people left out of the American dream.

It was not, however, a sudden theological shift that motivated Evangelical Christians to begin responding to the needs of poor people. As theological utopianism in the early 20th century was spawned by scientific and educational advances, so the new face of poverty in the mid-20th century demanded a response from Bible-believing Christians, as Evangelicals sometimes like to call themselves.

The Civil Rights Movement too was a wake-up call for Evangelicals, who along with the rest of society had ignored the sufferings of the largest minority in the nation. The urban riots of the '60s awakened a nation to the volatile and threatening unrest of minorities. Theological utopianism, which informed both Evangelical and liberal thought, ignored the plight of African-Americans. While social gospel advocates defended the rights of industrial workers, they all but ignored the economic injustice visited upon America's Black population. Even though they were overwhelmingly Evangelical Christians, African-Americans found few friends within the ranks of predominately white conservative churches.

While conservative churches were most often opposed to preachers who marched in defiance of legal segregation, the needs of Black people could no longer be ignored and would eventually begin to change attitudes about poverty. The incongruity of sending missionaries to Africa while ignoring the needs of people at home began to eat at the conscience of missionary-minded believers motivated by the Great Commission. If one understands that African-Americans are statistically at least as Christian as the majority community, the missionary analogy doesn't really apply. But the historic commitment of Evangelical Christianity to the missionary enterprise provided the practical motivation and explanation for a new response to people in need.

Carl F. H. Henry, one of the most respected Evangelical theologians of the recent past, called for Evangelical social concern in his 1947 book *The Uneasy Conscience of Modern Fundamentalism.*[7] While cautious by present standards, Henry in his many books and articles urged Evangelicals to assume responsibility for the care of society.

Senator Mark Hatfield, widely known among Evangelicals as a Christian politician, in 1971 wrote *Conflict and Conscience,* a compilation of speeches in which he took somewhat liberal views on issues of war and peace, poverty and wealth. In his later book, *Between a Rock and a Hard Place,* Hatfield lamented that the strongest opposition to his efforts to bring about justice through politics came from his fellow Evangelicals.[8]

These, along with other writers, were among the first to apply the biblical mandate to the social problems of the 20th century. But they didn't speak for the mainstream of conservative Evangelical thought. Even though softened by the growing unrest in the cities, Evangelicals continued to practice an evangelism driven by individualistic definitions of sin and salvation. The solution to society's ills was and remains for most Evangelical Christians simply the multiplication of converts. Efforts to change society are suspect, seen as misplaced if not unpatriotic.

It should be noted that for more than a century within Evangelical Christianity there have been two notable exceptions to withdrawal from social responsibility. The Salvation Army and gospel (or city) rescue missions, led and maintained primarily by Evangelical leaders, have always been in the forefront of a hands-on response to people in need.[9] The Salvation Army stands within the Wesleyan-Holiness Movement and is an active participant in the Christian Holiness Association. While the Army was in the recent past sometimes criticized by others within the Holiness Movement for abandoning evangelism, it remained true to its conservative Evangelical roots. Today the Salvation Army is the world's largest religious charitable organization.

The continuing presence of rescue missions is another example of direct service by Evangelicals to people in need. In an earlier time these missions were thought of primarily as way stations for transients or moral reprobates who were obviously suffering the consequences of their sins. Offering an opportunity for hungry men (few missions ever served women and children) to repent and believe before providing board and bed seemed a perfectly logical and Christian way both to respond to the immediate need and to solve the basic problem. That was before homelessness began to plague the cities. Every major city and many smaller towns have missions with a history of support among Evangelical Christians. Increasingly, they are responding to the needs of the chronically homeless, not only with overnight shelter but also with drug rehabilitation, job training, and life skills development programs. They have earned the respect of the general public for opening their doors to the street people of the cities, the urban nomads who make up the soft underbelly of urban culture.

As significant as the Salvation Army and the missions have been, they have remained around the edges of the Evangelical Movement. The relatively new interest in compassionate ministry in the Church of the Nazarene and the corresponding denominational and parachurch social activism within the broader Evangelical community come to the heart of things in local congregations. It has been from this grassroots, congregational interest that the newcomers to this evangelical response to people in need have come. Increasingly, members of local churches have formed nonprofit charitable organizations with a wide variety of ministries, including education, health care, and housing programs.

Compassionate ministry in the Church of the Nazarene, as social action among Evangelicals, has been more instinctive than intentional. In his book *The Vast Majority,* Michael Harrington claimed that most Americans are compassionate, that few would refuse to share their lunch with a hungry person before them.[10] A gnawing awareness of human need has forced sensitive Evangelicals to move from reaction to response.

1 ∽

Compassion Evangelism: The Right Focus

The question of how compassionate ministries and evangelism can coexist is being answered by new definitions of biblical compassion and New Testament evangelism. Words and actions merge into one gospel presentation.

In its most simple expression, compassion is a personal response to someone in need. While compassion can describe a ministry or a program, it is first a personal feeling toward the weak and unfortunate that leads to response. In the biblical tradition, compassion originated in the nature of God and was demonstrated in the life and teachings of Jesus.

Following the Israelites' fall into paganism, Moses feared for their future. They had rejected the unseen God of their liberation in order to worship a golden calf. In response to Moses' pleas, the presence of the Lord was revealed to him on Mount Sinai. Commandments were given and chiseled in stone, and a covenant was offered. The sins of the people were forgiven. The people were to know that reconciliation was made possible by One who chose to be known as "the compassionate and gracious God, slow to anger, abounding in love and faithfulness" (Exod. 34:6). (The reference "compassionate and gracious" appears in 11 other passages. It stands by itself in 5 of them.

It is linked with "slow to anger and rich in steadfast love," in 5 additional passages.[1])

The Hebrew word *rhm,* translated "compassion" in the Old Testament, is often translated as "mercy" in the New Testament. "While it yields many meanings, the term may refer to the deep love one has for another, usually the love of a superior for an inferior, that is rooted in some natural bond. It can also mean 'womb' and is frequently used to speak of a mother's love for her child."[2] It is likewise used to describe the nature of God as in the concluding verse of Luke's Sermon on the Plain, where mercy or compassion becomes the standard for the followers of Jesus: "Be merciful, just as your Father is merciful" (6:36).

The Gospels introduce another word used only to describe the compassion of Jesus. Jesus uses this word in the stories of the prodigal son and the Good Samaritan. The noun *splagchna,* from which *splanchnizomai* (compassion) is translated, literally means the heart, lungs, liver, kidney—the inward parts, or "bowels" as sometimes found in the King James Version. The word is intended to convey an identification with suffering that is so real that it produces physical effects. It's more than an intellectual understanding, deeper than our common understanding of sympathy. In contemporary expression we might say that compassion is to feel another's pain so deeply that it produces a "gut reaction."

Beyond this intense feeling for or with the weak and unfortunate, compassion as it is used to describe the ministry of Jesus always leads to action. It is more than empathy. It is a strong feeling and identification that produce a response to human need. Thus, Jesus told of a loving father extending compassion to a wayward son struggling to find his way home and a Samaritan traveling a foreign and hostile road, moved with compassion to care for a stranger robbed and left for dead. Stirred with compassion, He directed His disciples to serve the hungry multitude. Crowds were more than unnamed faces for Jesus. Compassion drew Him into the crowds of "harassed and helpless" people, touching and healing them one at a time (Matt. 9:35-38). Compassion keeps the gospel close to human need.

The biblical revelation of a compassionate God combined with the compassionate ministry of Jesus established the context for New Testament Christianity.

The noun "evangelism" does not occur in the New Testament. The root form "to evangelize" is a single Greek word best translated by the phrase "to proclaim good news." This Good News, the gospel of the New Testament, promised hope to first-century marginalized people trapped in insurmountable oppression. The gospel, however, was not "good news" to everyone. This is particularly clear in Luke 4, where Jesus began His ministry in the Nazareth synagogue by announcing His mission "to preach good news to the poor" (v. 18). Later on in the chapter, Luke reports that the people who heard the so-called good news dragged Jesus to the edge of the city, where they intended to kill Him. The gospel has a cutting edge. Those who heard it first understood clearly the threat Jesus' message held for those who gained their power and wealth at the expense of the poor and needy.

The people were soon to learn that spreading the Good News meant healing, feeding, teaching, and forgiving. The gospel was proclaimed in deeds as well as words. The weak and unfortunate were touched at the point of their need with the compassion of Jesus and were invited to become followers of Jesus. The good news of what Jesus was doing and saying was directed to people from all walks of life. Even the rich and powerful were offered freedom from the clutches of their materialism and invited to a life of service. But mostly the gospel was for the "harassed and helpless." It was among these marginalized unfortunates—sinners, beggars, and outcasts—that the Good News, the gospel, spread most rapidly. Evangelizing (or more literally "good newsing") people in the New Testament was unmistakably intended to meet the temporal, physical needs of people as well as to deal with matters of the heart.

From the days of Charles Finney and the 19th-century revivalists, evangelism has become narrowly defined as a way or technique of persuading nonbelievers to embrace Christianity. The content of the gospel became less important than the means of persuasion. This is expressed in the title of Marshall McLuhan's book, *The Medium Is the Message*.[3] The moment of conversion, with the expected (if not demanded) emotional religious experience, became the only acceptable rite of passage to the Christian community. The ethical expectations that accompanied this kind of evangelism were primarily confined to personal behavior. Nearly forgotten was evangelism in the New Testament context. Evangelism among present-day Evangelicals became, as Jim Wallis of the radical Sojourners group once called it, "evangelism without the gospel."[4] Evangelism of this sort would more appropriately be called "revivalism," describing a rather recent technique of proclaiming the gospel. Nazarenes may be surprised to know that John Wesley, a century before Finney, knew nothing of invitations and altar calls. Wesley's spiritual awakening, when his "heart was strangely warmed" while listening to someone read from Luther's preface to the Book of Romans, was hardly a camp meeting experience.

During the early 20th century, with the legacy of 19th-century revivalism, evangelism was reduced to a certain type of preaching. It became the special province of itinerate preachers invited by congregations for semiannual revivals. These men and women preachers were especially skilled in "drawing the net," persuading people to come forward to accept Christ. In the camp meetings and revivals of an earlier time, it was not unusual after the sermon to have an exhorter make the appeal. These exhorters were, as the evangelists of the mid-20th century, skilled at persuading converts to make public commitments.

By the middle of the 20th century, evangelism had taken on new forms. Billy Graham has much in common with mass evangelists Charles Finney (19th century) and Billy Sunday (early 20th century), but the televised Billy Graham Crusades and all the television evangelists to follow introduced a quantum leap in evangelistic persuasion. It would not be long before the most common image of an evangelist would be a television preacher with a national audience rather than a relatively obscure traveling preacher. At the other end of the spectrum, personal evangelism was promoted by Campus Crusade and James Kennedy's Evangelism Explosion. These one-to-one encounters were a way of increasing converts in a time when getting people to leave their television sets to attend a local church revival had become increasingly difficult. In all these methods of making converts, evangelism was separated from its full New Testament context of "good newsing" the poor and needy and challenging economic and political injustice.

Evangelicals may well defend their narrow perspective as an appropriate reaction to liberal Christianity, wherein evangelism has for the most part been reduced to social action. Indeed, the idea that social justice will automatically produce a corresponding improvement in personal behavior has been seriously questioned if not discredited. The great failure of modern society is technology and education without morality. There remains a need for those who believe in Christian missions to recover the biblical understanding of evangelism as both proclamation and service.

This is not to suggest that the evangelism or revivalism of the past century has been all wrong. It's been just half true. It is true that sin is personal, that each individual must experience a spiritual awakening if life is to have any promise or hope. It is also true that good people—saved and sanctified people, people filled with the Holy Spirit—can be reduced to poverty and suffering through no fault of their own. It is true that much suffering in our society and in underdeveloped countries is self-inflicted and is the predictable consequence of irresponsible and immoral living. It is also true that much of the wealth hoarded by the rich has been accumulated at the expense of the poor.

New Testament good news or evangelism does not guarantee wealth. It does promise believers the inner spiritual resources needed to survive with faith when surrounded by suffering. If prosperity comes, it bears an accompanying responsibility of stewardship. Evangelism always calls for a responsible use of the material resources entrusted by God into the hands of people called to build the Kingdom.

In a similar way, merging compassion and evangelism will redefine our understanding of righteousness. Righteousness among Evangelicals has become almost synonymous with personal piety. To be "righteous" is to avoid the commonly understood sins of personal behavior. This definition has unfortunately defined Evangelical Christians by what they don't do rather than by any positive identifiable morality, let alone social responsibility.

The Hebrew and Greek words translated in the English Bible by the word "righteousness" could just as accurately be translated "justice." The "righteousness of God" so often referred to in Romans, for instance, describes not simply a world where individuals refrain from personal sins, but also a world in which the structures of society are shaped to promote the ideals of the kingdom of God. For the apostle Paul, as well as the Gospel writers and the Hebrew prophets, "righteousness" meant an end to public injustice and oppression.

A theology that informs and encourages compassionate ministry and redefines evangelism and righteousness will recover a balance between the personal and social dimensions of the gospel. During the era of retrenchment, the biblical mandate to serve as well as witness, to seek justice as well as personal morality, was distorted and blurred. There remained in the Wesleyan tradition, however, a certain optimism about the possibilities of personal and social transformation. The followers of John Wesley in Methodism, the Salvation Army, and the Holiness Movement have been optimistic about the possibilities for change. Wesley believed people as well as society could and should be transformed.

This optimism about the possibilities of a spiritual awakening continues to produce a distinctive kind of social action. People in need are not reduced to problems or lumped together as statistics. While Evangelicals involved in social or compassionate ministries will deal with the macro issues of public policy along with everyone else, they will concentrate always and primarily upon the welfare of the individual. Whether the person in need is the victim or the victimizer, or some combination of the two, compassionate ministry will always offer faith in Jesus as Lord as the Source of strength needed to survive, even to overcome the struggles of life.

While it is true that authentic evangelists and evangelistic programs have always been bathed in an atmosphere of Christian compassion, it is also true that too often evangelists and evangelistic programs have not intentionally committed themselves to a ministry of meeting human or temporal needs. Compassionate ministry does not denigrate the spoken gospel word nor diminish the importance of presenting the claims of personal salvation. To the contrary, responding to temporal needs opens the door for sharing the faith.

As it is possible to have evangelism without responding to the temporal or physical needs of those to whom the gospel is presented, so it is that many programs that address social problems are conducted without evangelism. There is a secular form of compassion that makes no attempt to address the inner spiritual needs of people. Compassion is a human response seen in everyday deeds of kindness. If some people are inclined to evil, so many are also inspired to goodness and altruism. Not many of us would eat our lunch without sharing with a hungry person. While it is possible to meet human need without the gospel, it is not possible to proclaim the gospel without meeting human need. Compassion evangelism goes beyond the normal acts of kindness.

In the teachings of Jesus, compassion includes generosity to the ungrateful, even forgiveness for enemies. And it recognizes the inner suffering of loneliness and guilt. If compassion leads Jesus to feed the hungry, it also provides the bread of life—food for the soul. When Jesus heals, He also restores inner well-being.

Responding only to the temporal needs of people—healing, feeding, housing—is not enough. Broken and burdened people need the inner resources only faith can provide. In a world that does not always reward the faithful, some people, no matter how good they are or how hard they try, will suffer. Compassion will not always remove misfortune. Those who serve in Jesus' name seldom have all the resources needed to meet overwhelming human need. The good news represented by the life of Jesus is ultimately about a God who suffers with us, becoming like us even in death.

Compassion and evangelism—two words that, when joined together, bring us close to the essential ministry and message of Jesus. It's not that compassionate evangelism is a new technique added to our traditional evangelistic strategies. Nor is compassion a means to an end. Christian compassion is a sign of the Kingdom, never to be reduced to an act or a program designed for show or effect.

I remember when one of our Community of Hope members was asked, "How many souls have been saved by your influence?" The question, from a somewhat skeptical visitor, was intended to evaluate our ministry from the perspective of what was assumed to be the primary evangelistic mission of the church. It is not unusual for the question to be raised. Is compassionate ministry really contributing to the primary mission of the church?

That question is continually asked of Nazarene Compassionate Ministries in one form or another. While ministries of mercy to people in need are widely supported as something the church should be doing, especially when natural disaster strikes, such activity is also thought of by some as separate from the church's primary evangelistic and missionary mandate. If, of course, it can be demonstrated that compassionate ministry (service to the economically disadvantaged and distressed) leads to evangelism (a means to an end), then all is well.

The Community of Hope member answered: "I don't know for sure, but I know my own soul has been saved." I know him well enough to be sure that he was, and is, as committed to the personal dimensions of the gospel as anyone. But at that moment he expressed something central to the Christian faith. Good deeds are expressions of, or the result of, our faith. Serving needy people was a calling for him. It was what we might call a "sign of the Kingdom." He wasn't trying to earn favor with God or work his way to heaven—this was not works righteousness. His service was a simple expression of what he understood it meant to be a follower of Jesus.

Compassionate ministries have thrived in the Church of the Nazarene in part because they were central to the ministries of John Wesley in the 18th-century Evangelical Revival and Phineas F. Bresee, founder of the Church of the Nazarene around the beginning of the 20th century. Both men felt called specifically to serve the poor. Both were evangelists and social reformers. Yet I suspect they would have a difficult time understanding the way we have distinguished between evangelism and compassionate ministries. The differences have much to do with the rise of theological modernism and Fundamentalism in the early 20th century. The result is that in the minds of many church members today, evangelism and compassionate ministry are so narrowly understood they have little to do with one another. In their minds, evangelism addresses the inner spiritual needs of people, while compassionate ministries comprise a response to the temporal needs of the weak and unfortunate.

While we can't go back to the days of Wesley and Bresee, we must apply the same biblical mandate to the needs of our own times. If we aren't more careful with the definition of the church's mission and the consequent development of programs, we may miss the opportunities as well as the obligations of ministry as we near the 21st century. At a more practical level, in a time of scarce resources, the rising interest in compassionate ministries could become divisive if not seen as an integral and essential part of the church's mission.

I have a camera with a built-in range finder. It's somewhat obsolete—from before the days of automatic focusing mechanisms. As I look through the viewer, I see two circles I can overlay by turning the lens. When the circles converge on the subject I want to photograph, the camera is properly focused. I've thought of evangelism and compassion as two circles essential to the Christian faith. When our faith is in focus, it is difficult, if not impossible, to distinguish one from the other.

The boat with two oars or the bird with two wings is sometimes used as a metaphor for the need of both evangelism and compassion. With just one oar the boat goes in circles. With only one wing the bird can't fly. As helpful as these illustrations are, they are limited, reflecting a less-than-informed biblical anthropology. An early distortion of the Christian faith was to see the world and people as essentially divided between the spiritual and physical. The Judeo-Christian tradition sees human life as one, or holistic, with the physical and spiritual merged into one complete being. From the creation story we understand that human life begins when a physical body is infused with the breath of God. The biblical themes of evangelism and compassion reflect this truth.

Compassion is used as often, if not more often, than

any other word to describe the nature of God in the Old Testament. As mentioned earlier in the chapter, the phrase describing God as "compassionate and gracious" appears in Exod. 34:6 and in several other passages. If we bring to this verse only the common narrow understanding of compassionate ministries as a response to physical or temporal needs, we miss the meaning of the text. As Dianne Bergant, in her article "Compassion in the Bible," writes, "Compassion is the disposition God shows to repentant sinners."[5] Clearly, compassion here expresses God's concern for more than the physical well-being of His people.

In the prodigal son story, the loving father had "compassion" for the wayward younger son making his way home (Luke 15:20). While the son was destitute, the story is meant to express God's loving acceptance of the spiritually lost as much as to offer shelter for a homeless profligate. The son's physical and spiritual needs converge.

The same word translated "compassion" is used in Luke 10 to describe the Good Samaritan (v. 33, KJV). Compassionate ministry activists themselves have sometimes applied this story out of context. The Good Samaritan story is usually used to describe an act of altruism without a response to spiritual needs. The unnamed Samaritan responded to a person he had never seen and would have no reason to see again. There seemed to be no opportunity to respond to anything other than the emergency physical wounds of the victim. But that interpretation takes the story out of context and misses the primary point Jesus made in the telling.

The Good Samaritan story was told in response to a question about finding eternal life. It wasn't told to promote random acts of kindness, as it is sometimes used when we refer to people who spontaneously reach out to help others as "good Samaritans." As worthy as such acts are, there is a deeper meaning plainly revealed in the context. Before Jesus finished the story, He instructed the religious teacher who began the discussion to "do this and you will live" (Luke 10:28). To "live" in this instance meant to have eternal life.

Jesus was responding to the need of the religious teacher standing before him asking a question about finding eternal life. The need of the man left to die and the response of the Samaritan are part of an illustration used to lead a person to eternal life. It was with compassion that Jesus responded to the interrogator, as it was compassion that motivated the Samaritan. The two circles of evangelism and compassion merge. The gospel is in clear focus.

In Matt. 9:35-38, while preaching, teaching, and healing in the synagogues and streets of Galilee, Jesus is described as having compassion for the crowds, "harassed and helpless, like sheep without a shepherd" (v. 36). It's clear that the word "compassion" is used to describe all that Jesus was doing. Compassion was expressed in the good news of the message just as it was in His gracious acts of healing.

In the writings of the apostle Paul, particularly in Romans, the implications of the "gospel" as the "power of God for the salvation of everyone who believes" are fully developed (1:16). In this most theological of New Testament writings, one might wonder what compassionate ministry has to do with the lengthy discussions about sin, salvation, and sanctification. But in Romans 12 the two circles converge again, bringing the gospel message into focus. As the spiritual gifts necessary for ministry are listed, along with preaching and teaching are the gifts of "contributing to the needs of others" and "showing mercy," a synonym for compassion (v. 8). Some of the following verses directing charity even to one's enemies sound like direct quotations from the Sermon on the Mount.

Compassion and its synonym "mercy" are biblical descriptions of the divine disposition that motivated God to offer the covenant through Moses to the Israelites and the gospel through Jesus to all people. Because God is compassionate, the good news of the Kingdom is proclaimed. To evangelize is to announce that a compassionate God has offered grace (undeserved love) and is calling followers to help fulfill the promises of a better life in this world through the coming of the Kingdom, "on earth as it is in heaven" (Matt. 6:10).

Things got out of focus among some of the first Christians. The early chapters of Acts describe a Christian community of multiplying converts where believers were meeting daily for prayer and fellowship; even "selling their possessions and goods, they gave to anyone as he had need" (2:45). Again Acts 4:34 records the practice of selling houses and lands when needed to meet the needs of the impoverished among them. No wonder people flocked to their ministries.

In the excitement and rush of activity with so many new disciples, it was brought to the attention of the apostles that the Greek "widows were being overlooked in the daily distribution of food" (6:1). The apostles knew the gospel required both the ministry of the Word and waiting on tables (v. 2). While they would devote themselves to "prayer and the ministry of the word" (v. 4), they also said, "We will turn this responsibility" (waiting on tables) to others "full of the Spirit and wisdom" (v. 3). Stephen, the first Christian martyr, was among these Greek leaders whom the Early Church ordained, by the laying on of hands and prayer, to the essential work of caring for indigent widows.

The letter of James was written in part to get the focus right. Here the two circles are described as faith and deeds. When compassionate deeds are left out of the Christian community, faith is dead—a meaningless abstraction. James asks a series of penetrating rhetorical questions. "What good is it, my brothers, if a man claims to have faith but has no deeds? Can such faith save him?" (2:14). The "deeds" referred to are what we might call compassionate ministry—feeding and clothing the poor and needy. He pushes the question: "If one of you says to him, 'Go, I wish you well; keep warm and well fed,' but does nothing about his physical needs, what good is it?" (v. 16).

These are not isolated references. In 1 John 3:17 the rhetorical question is even stronger. "If anyone has material possessions and sees his brother in need but has no pity on him, how can the love of God be in him?" Throughout Scripture the message is clear: it is only when evangelism and compassion combine, so that they represent an integrated mission, that the gospel is in focus.

It would not have occurred to either Wesley or Bresee to organize "compassionate ministries" apart from the primary emphasis of their ministries. Responding to the physical, temporal needs of people who were likely to be found in the churches of their times *was* the mission. Among the illiterate and impoverished industrial workers of England's major cities and the street people of the inner city of Los Angeles is where these two leaders established their ministries. Each of them and their followers preached and waited on tables and did a lot of other things to be sure that needy people were welcomed and supported.

But things have gotten out of focus again. Sometime in the mid-20th century the spiritual descendants of Bresee and Wesley, reacting to those who sought to reduce Christianity to social action, became as one-sided as those they criticized. In their zeal to multiply converts, compassionate deeds were not included in the church's primary mission. Some went so far as to suggest that any Christian response to the physical needs of the weak and unfortunate is at least a distraction from, if not a distortion of, the essential gospel message. Evangelism, the Good News, was reduced to the promise of better times in the world to come. It held little regard for the urgent needs of the vast majority of the world's people for the basics of food, shelter, and clothing, and the resources to build better lives and neighborhoods.

For more than a generation now the church's mission has been out of focus. For a while the circle of compassion wasn't in the picture at all. Only recently have we begun to realize there is another essential element in the church's mission. We are just beginning to realize further that evangelism and compassion are not two different and separate biblical prerogatives. Nazarene Compassionate Ministries has emerged in the very recent past from a grassroots realization that wherever there is human need, the gospel mandate requires response.

Compassionate ministries, or compassion evangelism, is helping get the picture in focus again. If there are some who are not sure how compassionate ministries translates into or merges with evangelism, there may be others who are not sure that evangelism has much to do with compassionate ministries. It is clearly no longer an either/or choice—evangelism or compassionate ministries. It's both/and—compassion and evangelism together in one integrated mission.

Compassion evangelism has been suggested as a definition of the church's mission in a hurting and desperate world. It's an attempt to harmonize our words and deeds with the biblical message of compassion and good news. We can be thankful now that when we look through the lens of a camera, we see two circles that are beginning to converge. With continued faithfulness to the ministry to which we have all been called, we can get it in focus again.

Compassionate Ministries is an organized effort to fulfill Luke 6:36—"Be merciful, just as your Father is merciful," extending God's compassion in deeds of kindness and justice. It is also the bread of life for the hungry hearts. Compassionate ministry is truly biblical when it extends forgiveness and grace even as it touches people at the point of their physical and temporal needs. Likewise, evangelism as commonly understood is true to the gospel only when it is as sensitive to physical and temporal distress as to a hungry heart.

2 ❧

Reading the Bible from the Streets

Compassion evangelism is about reading the Bible through the eyes of the poor. It's about demonstrating theology in the mean streets. It's incarnation and resurrection.

Good news for George

I was doing my best to persuade a homeless man to come in and worship with us at the Community of Hope. It was a bitterly cold winter day. Not many people were on the street that morning.

"George," I called, "I have some good news for you." I was thinking of the message I had prepared from Luke 4. George refused my invitation, saying something about not being well enough dressed to attend church, even though most of the people attending were not that well dressed either.

After the service I was standing alone on the front steps of the old apartment building that housed our chapel and heard George calling to me from the sidewalk: "Tom, what was that good news you had for me?"

I knew immediately that he had waited around to hear about what I might have had in mind. He obviously didn't assume I was talking about a sermon! I knew he was sleeping in an abandoned, burnt-out building across the street. He told me he was hungry *and cold. The only good news for George would be the promise of food and shelter from the cold.*

Eventually I came to know much more about him, including the fact that he was illiterate. But if I could have explained to him the meaning of the Good News, the gospel of Jesus to the poor and needy, his expectation would have been closer to the truth than the words I preached as he stood outside, cold and hungry, even as we worshiped in comfort and warmth.

According to the Gospel of Luke, chapter 4, Jesus began His ministry with a dramatic announcement during a Sabbath synagogue service among His family and friends in His hometown of Nazareth. When given the opportunity to read the Scripture, the scroll was opened to the Book of the ancient prophet Isaiah, chapter 61, where Jesus read as follows:

The Spirit of the Lord is on me,
  because he has anointed me
  to preach good news to the poor.
He has sent me to proclaim freedom for the prisoners
  and recovery of sight for the blind,
  to release the oppressed,
  to proclaim the year of the Lord's favor.

—Luke 4:18-19

And then came His bold claim that turned an ordinary group of Sabbath worshipers into a vicious mob:

"Today this scripture is fulfilled in your hearing" (v. 21).

There followed an impromptu discussion with the people challenging Jesus. They couldn't believe that a young man they had known since childhood would have the audacity to make such a claim for himself. Jesus retorted, comparing them to the unbelieving Israelites during the time of Elijah.

Confusion forced an end to the service. They drove Jesus out of the synagogue and dragged Him through the streets to a cliff, where the congregation attempted to hurl Him to His death. One can only wonder what was going on to enrage a congregation to such fury. There is obviously more here than meets the eye.

This calling to "preach good news to the poor" meant much more than preparing sermons for worship. Jesus stepped forward at that moment claiming to be the One anointed by the Spirit to inaugurate a new day of social as well as personal righteousness and justice.

In the reading from Isaiah 61, Jesus repeated verses understood as a prophetic vision of a time when the Messiah would lead the people of Israel out of their misery. The prophets revived the earliest recollections of God's will for His people, indeed *all* people, as recorded in the statutes given to Moses for a just society. If society was to be ordered as directed by God according to the laws of Moses, no one would get too rich or too poor. Leviticus 25 describes a series of regulations known as the "jubilee laws," named after the central idea of the jubilee or the Sabbath year, when these regulations would take effect.

The word "jubilee" is a near-literal translation of the Hebrew word for the ram's horn, *yobel,* used to trumpet the ceremony announcing the beginning of the year of jubilee. The jubilee year was celebrated every 50 years. Just as the week ended with a Sabbath day and the week of years (seven years) ended with a sabbatical year, each period of 49 years ended with the jubilee.

The four primary provisions of the jubilee were (1) letting the land lie fallow, (2) the remitting of debts, (3) the liberation of slaves, and (4) the redistribution of capital. Allowing the land to lie fallow was the only provision practiced with any degree of regularity. For the most part the ideals of Leviticus 25 were ignored until renewed by the prophetic vision of an age when the Messiah, the one anointed by the Spirit, would restore economic justice for everyone by implementing this ancient code of personal and social ethics.

The "year of the Lord's favor," the jubilee, would mean freedom from want and release from oppressive debt and disadvantage. This is what Jesus promised. Those who challenged Him in the synagogue knew exactly what the fulfillment of this promise meant. The gospel was obviously not good news for everyone. If this concept was to become a reality, none of them would be able to hoard unnecessary wealth in the presence of unmet human need.

All of that was going through my mind as I met George at the close of our worship and my sermon on "Good News." When George asked about that good news, I knew exactly what he meant. He was expecting that I might be able to help him find shelter and food, that he too might live through the day and night.

We really didn't have an adequate place at the Community of Hope. Our building was undergoing renovations so that we could fulfill our vision of making it a place of refuge for homeless families. George had no family, and he couldn't wait. A room was found. That night's lodging stretched into more than a year while he struggled to get his life together.

The morning papers the next day carried the tragic announcement of two nameless men like George who didn't survive. They died from the cold, sleeping in the alleys and abandoned buildings of the nation's capital.

That overarching biblical vision of righteousness still inspires people to follow Jesus in repeating the announcement. Isaiah 61 was a favorite scripture of both John Wesley and Phineas Bresee, two men who heard for themselves a call to "preach good news to the poor." For each of them, responding to the temporal and spiritual needs of poor people was not a tangent.

John Wesley, the founder of Methodism in 18th-century England, inspired a movement that included William and Catherine Booth, the founders of the Salvation Army, and Phineas Bresee, who organized the first Nazarene church—a turn-of-the-century inner-city mission in Los

Angeles. For all these people, their Holiness theology expressed the gospel mandate to respond to the poor. Compassionate ministry was more than one effort among many. In their estimation, it was central to the gospel message. They would never separate "to preach good news" from "to the poor." As Wesley said, if the rich hear the Word and follow Jesus, fine. But his ministry, as the gospel mandate, was primarily "good news to the poor."

What are you going to do about it?

I had come upon an angry crowd warned to keep their distance from a drug bust. The "jump-out squad," plainclothes police officers known for their tactics of surprise and intimidation, pinned a young man from the neighborhood facedown on the sidewalk, his hands handcuffed behind his back. A woman was screaming at a large, burly officer who was wielding a baseball bat. Evidently there had been quite a struggle making the arrest.

I moved up to observe more closely. Some of the officers recognized me as a minister and knew my organization was as concerned with police brutality as with crime prevention. The woman cried out at the police, "This is my son—he wasn't doing anything!" She was beside herself as she watched her teenaged boy being knocked to the ground, handcuffed, and eventually taken away for investigation.

Frustrated and enraged, she turned to me. She knew me only as a minister in the neighborhood. "What are you going to do about it?"—a question that in some way defines ministry in the inner city, or anywhere, for that matter.

She assumed that as a representative of the church, I bore some responsibility for the injustice she believed victimized her son. It didn't matter that she was not a member of my congregation or that I had never seen her son. Something was wrong. The church, and I in particular, could not evade our calling to challenge injustice.

Whether we like it, or even realize it, as followers of Jesus we are expected to do something about the critical issues facing society, particularly the plight of people in need. In a sense we do not have the luxury of defining our mission.

Centuries ago the prophet Jeremiah conveyed a surprising challenge to the Israelites held captive in Babylon. "Seek the peace and prosperity of the city to which I have carried you into exile. Pray to the LORD for it, because if it prospers, you too will prosper" (29:7). The translators here have used the phrase "peace and prosperity" to interpret the meaning of the Hebrew word *shalom.* We might just as well read the verse as follows: "Seek the shalom of the city to which I have carried you into exile. Pray to the LORD for it, because if it finds shalom, you too will find shalom."

Shalom means more than the absence of hostility or simply a live-and-let-live attitude. It means the harmonious working together of all the people and systems of society. Whether these captive Israelites liked it or not, their lives were intertwined with the lives of their oppressors. Even as they held fast to their faith and longed to return to their own land, they were to be a redemptive presence where they were at that moment. That had to sound impossibly naive to those who first heard it. Why should the people of God work for the good of the city in which they were being held in exile?

We might wonder that also when we think of our own cities. Why should anyone feel responsibility for the crime and violence, the unemployment and poverty, the sickness and death destroying cities and their people? For a generation and more, those who could afford it have left modern American cities. We drive around the inner-city neighborhoods if we can. If we cannot, we lock our doors and hurry on.

The exiles were not to endure their misfortune as pawns in international conflict. They were not even to blame their captors. Babylon was to be for them "the city to which I have carried you into exile." As unreasonable as it must have seemed to them, there was a redemptive purpose in the heartache of captivity.

Jeremiah reminded the exiles that as difficult as it might be for them, they must work for the best interests of the city. They would enjoy their own safety and security only in a stable, peaceful society. Building barriers would not work. They couldn't retreat far enough to escape the consequences of a chaotic city. Sooner or later they would go down with the others unless shalom prevailed in Babylon.

We might call this enlightened self-interest. Yet I'm sure selfishness was not the motive. Jeremiah reminded the exiles of an inescapable fact of life for people of any city in any age. We are all inextricably intertwined in a human family. Sooner or later, what affects one affects all. Salvation is not just a personal relationship with the Lord. The Israelites' salvation was dependent to some degree on how well the whole city fared. Likewise in our society, we simply cannot afford the cost of millions of marginalized people—if for no other reason than that the prosperity of everyone is dependent upon providing opportunities to escape the cycle of poverty. It is not enough to relieve the poor with philanthropy or to secure the peace with force. The community, the unity the people of God seek, can be realized only as they work for the community and unity, the shalom, of the Babylons of this age.

In a series of books by Old Testament scholar Walter Brueggemann, we are reminded that the exiles never forgot their identity as they worked for the peace of Babylon. They did not become Babylonians. They always knew who they were as the people of God in exile. Brueggemann sees the Exile as an apt analogy or paradigm for Christians today, especially those who venture into the city to serve in Jesus' name.

We should not underestimate the destructiveness of the evil and violence of the city even as we work for its welfare. Yet as we would not embrace the materialistic and self-destructive culture of urban society, neither can we run from it. Jesus described His followers as the salt and leaven that, in some unseen yet noticeable way, preserves the whole society. A strange calling—to preserve and work for the stability of a city and society we often abhor.

The exiles were not to endure their misfortune as pawns in international conflict. As difficult as it might have seemed to them, there was a redemptive purpose in the heartache of captivity. Even today the task of rebuilding the "ruined cities" (Isa. 61:4; Amos 9:14) is not a burden to be borne by reluctant disciples. Compassionate ministry is a calling. Reaching out to people in need, the victimizers as well as the victims, is the work of God in society. Responding to human need, praying for shalom, is more than a responsibility—it is our opportunity to cooperate with God's wider purposes for all mankind.

> *I was not an innocent bystander to the woman who screamed at me as she protested to the police on behalf of her son. If that neighborhood was to be overcome with violence, whether from the criminals or police, no one would be safe. I understood as I walked away that I could not escape to the suburbs. Violence would follow. And it has.*

Who cares?

> *"God must have brought me into the world to suffer!" cried a young, homeless mother with five children in tow. She came to us years ago, before family homelessness was common in America's cities. It seemed to her that all the troubles of the world had converged in her miserable experience. She was surrounded by children she loved but didn't want, addicted to drugs she hated yet couldn't resist, and attracted to men who abused her. She never knew her father.*

When just 11, her childhood ended when she watched an intruder murder her mother.

If no one in her world of struggle and disappointment was able to help, it seemed unlikely to her that God cared. "If there is a God . . . ," she would often begin a sentence. Her story and lament has become all too familiar to me now as hundreds of desperate, homeless families have stood in line for our temporary emergency apartments. The situations change, the words vary, but the question coming from the streets of the city remains: "Who cares?"

For 20 years my view of the street was from a turn-of-the-century apartment building renovated as a place of worship and refuge for needy people in the heart of Washington, D.C.'s, inner northwest ghetto. In the background was the dome of the Capitol and the historic buildings that house the Supreme Court and the Library of Congress. I didn't have to go far to see the Washington, Lincoln, and Jefferson Monuments surrounded by tour buses and visitors. These symbols of America's democratic freedoms and material prosperity embody the dreams of Americans everywhere and still attract visitors from around the world.

That was the background to a very different foreground. On the streets beneath my window, a couple of miles north of the White House, lived people whom one of my minister friends called "the last, the lost, and the least"—people who were particularly important to Jesus. Inner-city neighborhoods like this have been described as "hypersegregated," crowded with people isolated by both race and poverty. Soon after I began my ministry there, a *Washington Post* reporter toured this part of town and wrote it off as a "pit stop on the way to hell."

Prior to the urban riots of the late 1960s, a vibrant business district stood on the vacant lots beside the building that houses the Community of Hope. The burned-out buildings were eventually leveled. Chain-link fences now secure the barren lots, while politicians and neighbor-hood special-interest groups argue about how to "renew the ruined cities," as the prophet Isaiah put it (61:4). Twenty-five years later, the land still lies vacant.

The human tragedy of poor and marginalized people struggling to survive in the shadow of, in fact next door to, the wealth and power of the Western world is the picture I saw every day from this window. In spite of all the govern-ment's late-20th-century social programs—the Great Soci-ety, the War on Poverty, urban renewal, and enterprise zones—not much has changed for the better. Some things are worse.

As recently as the early 1980s no one could have pre-dicted the proliferation of crack cocaine, leaving in its wake a tide of human wreckage—"boarder babies," teens gunning one another down with automatic weapons, en-tire neighborhoods held hostage to local drug dealers, and corrupt police officers.

Ten years ago AIDS (*a*cquired *i*mmuno*d*eficiency *s*yndrome) was unheard of. Even now as the AIDS threat seems to have abated somewhat among middle-class people, it rushes with frightening speed through minority inner-city neighborhoods. Some suggest that AIDS may no longer be seen as a national crisis, since its victims are primarily urban nomads—the men, women, and children who reside in what Phineas Bresee described as the "for-gotten quarters of the city."

There are signs that society has begun to tolerate the presence of a "permanent underclass," a "culture of pover-ty," a new strain of poverty resistant to any cure. Compas-sion fatigue sets in when homelessness, violence, and plagues defy our best efforts and threaten our limited re-sources. Otherwise informed Christians are occasionally heard to accept as inevitable that lives will be destroyed and wasted by poverty with a cavalier misinterpreted quote from Jesus: "The poor you will always have with you" (Matt. 26:11).

The Gospels speak often of the compassion of Jesus. In Matthew's account, as Jesus walked through the towns, He described people in need as "harassed and helpless, like sheep without a shepherd" (9:36). In our vernacular, we might describe them as oppressed people, of little or no concern to the leaders of society. The Word says that when He saw them, He was filled with compassion (vv. 35-38).

The poor of Jesus' time were as desperate and threatening as they are to us. Everywhere He went, Jesus seemed to attract crowds of marginalized people. In His time, the beggars were diseased and handicapped people with no choice but to beg for food. Women divorced by their husbands were disgraced, often forced into prostitution. There were no hospitals or public institutions to care for the weak and vulnerable. All these, including lepers, were further disadvantaged by a cruel theology that condemned people because of their problems.

When most self-reliant people ignored, if not berated, the poor because of their poverty, Jesus was moved with compassion to respond to their physical as well as their spiritual needs. Even more, He saw them as the ones most likely to follow His teachings. They were like a "field . . . white . . . to harvest," a golden opportunity for His disciples, who were instructed to "pray" for "labourers" to "harvest," or take advantage of the opportunity for the Kingdom represented by poor and needy people (John 4:35; Luke 10:2, KJV).

Later, in Matthew 14, the word "compassion" (v. 14) describes Jesus' response to an unexpectedly large crowd who stayed with His teaching so long that they were faint with hunger. The disciples knew their meager lunches would not go far among several thousand men, women, and children, so they wanted to send them away. "They do not need to go away," said Jesus. "You give them something to eat" (v. 16). Then the miracle occurred.

The word "compassion" in these passages translates a root Greek word with the literal meaning of "inward parts." "Pity" is a poor translation. Jesus was filled with anything but pity or condescension for disenfranchised people. He healed and fed them even as He condemned those who were content to hoard wealth in the presence of human need. When they used this word, the Greeks expressed the idea that compassion can produce a physical effect. As cited earlier in chapter 1, compassion can actually be felt in the "inward parts"—the stomach, the liver, or, as the King James Version translates it, even in the "bowels" (Phil. 2:1).

The unusual kindness of the unnamed Samaritan, from a despised racial and religious minority group, was singled out by Jesus as an example of the gospel (Luke 10:25 ff.). What a contrast to the professional religious people who "passed by on the other side" (vv. 31, 32)!

I remember another mother who came by years later after we had organized a program to house homeless families. She came upon us by accident, walking the streets with three children. She saw the sign over the entrance, Community of Hope, and walked in with no idea what kind of organization this was. She thought she was losing her mind, running from an abusive, drug-addicted husband, hiding to protect her children. "I needed both community and hope," she said. "As soon as I walked in, somebody put her arms around me." That was the beginning of her personal resurrection.

Her husband followed and eventually found her. Though he threatened her again, he too was touched with the compassion of Jesus and recovered from the insanity of drugs. They were reconciled and together became followers of Jesus. They found jobs at the Community of Hope, secured affordable housing, and began to touch others with the compassion of Jesus.

That's evangelism—touching people at the point of their need with the compassion of Jesus and inviting them to become His followers. Or as someone described it, evangelism is one beggar telling another where to find food.

Talking about Jesus

My grandmother was always talking about Jesus. And she always taught me the gospel. The Jesus she taught me about cared for those who were hungry and cared for those who were homeless and naked. I would go to churches and didn't have the proper clothes and felt I couldn't communicate well and couldn't verbalize what I was thinking. I always knew that I wasn't worthy. So I always felt that one day, when I got my life perfect, I would go to those churches and show them. But I would still be sitting in that abandoned building behind a locked door if I hadn't seen Jesus at work through the volunteers who were coming here from the church.

The church on Belmont Street has influenced me personally to the point where—and I think I can speak for my neighbors and some of my friends—the influence has been to love Jesus and then love one another. Once I got a taste of God's love and the love of Christ and realized exactly, and learned to know, how Christ died for me and died for my sins, I couldn't help but love the Lord. Once you love the Lord, you can't help but love people and give that love back.

Those are words from Rita Bright, a person I shouldn't have met. She was the last survivor in an old building ready to be condemned and boarded up. We thought we were buying an empty building to renovate eventually for our ministry on Belmont Street. But there she was with no place to go. This building, this street had been her home since early childhood. Now a young welfare mother with two children, she was certain she had reached the end of the road. She stayed. We got acquainted.

We knew that to succeed in its mission, the Community of Hope would have to build upon residents in the neighborhood. We also wondered whether or not they would choose to remain in such a distressed neighborhood and support the ministry once they were able to break the cycle of poverty by completing an education and getting jobs. If people were really helped as we wanted, would they stay or leave?

I always thought God blesses us and that if God blesses you, then you're supposed to "move on and be successful." And being successful means obtaining things. I thought once I moved up and acquired the skills that allowed me to acquire a house and move out of the neighborhood—that would be my final success. But lo and behold, moving out of the neighborhood was not what God meant for me to do.

The battle on Belmont Street seems to be so hopeless. People still feel they can't accomplish anything. And I think the battle is to bring Christ to more people. And I just know that once people get a taste of the Lord and really transform their lives and give their lives to Christ, they will be new creatures.

The church should look like ministry. The church should be a place where people can come and find love no matter what, under any circumstances. People who feel broken, who feel helpless, who feel they will not be accepted anyplace else, by society or by the world, will be accepted by the church. Like I always tell people who tell me they can't come to church because they still do drugs or they still smoke or they still drink—I just tell them, "I don't see you sitting in the doctor's office when you're well. I see you in the doctor's office when you have a problem. And the church is a place that should be there to help you get well. Should be a place where we will minister to you, along with the Lord, to help you get to the place where you need to be, and God will do the rest."

Rita helped us keep it together. She could never understand the problem of combining the personal and social dimensions of the gospel. As she began to study the Scriptures with us, it was plain to her that social activism and salvation were both necessary for ministry in the neighborhood. We had to respond to the obvious needs around us. But we had to do it in a way that offered faith, without which the people couldn't maintain the daily struggle for survival in this inner-city neighborhood.

We can house people and do all those things, but we always have to keep the gospel in there—they must go hand in hand. You can't hand out food without handing out Jesus. You can't house people without telling them about the Lord. And you can't clothe them without telling where those clothes came from. They always have to go hand in hand. We really have to look at helping people transform their lives now—right here on earth—to be a better person. Once you start loving the Lord, you start loving people, and you start loving yourself. You start caring.

Because I know for myself: I was provided with housing, health care, education, and employment; but until I really got involved in the church and really got involved in ministry—and what ministry and church should be all about—it was then that I found the Jesus that my grandmother talked about: the Jesus who housed people, fed people, who cared, who cried for people, who wept for our cities.

That's the Jesus I wanted to know, and that's the Jesus I wanted to walk with and draw closer to. And I just pray that anybody I come in contact with sees a little bit of that Jesus in me.

3 ❧

The Mission of the Church

The shape of the church must be determined by its mission. Compassionate ministry is as much about renewal as meeting human need.

The practitioners of Nazarene Compassionate Ministries have not waited for theologians to articulate a rationale for meeting human need. The biblical mandate is clear enough. Neither have they depended upon denominational programs or financial support to begin. In the mid-1970s, when some of the first compassionate ministry programs emerged, there was little or no coordination between denominational leaders and those who wanted to respond to human need from within church structures.[1]

Those who began these ministries hardly anticipated the widespread interest and support that came from nearly every sector of the Christian community. Major changes in the way Christians thought about church and society evolved quietly and surfaced to the surprise of many.

The changes have to do in part with the rise to prominence of conservative, Evangelical Christianity in the United States. Through the middle of the 20th century, mainline denominations dominated organized religion. As these groups began to lose members, conservative Evangelical denominations increased in size and influence. Evangelicals gained a sense of confidence in their own agenda, no longer simply reacting to liberals. The social gospel stigma that usually succeeded in frightening

Evangelicals away from social concern was for the most part forgotten. A generation of baby boomers, born after the controversies between liberalism and Fundamentalism, became increasingly critical of overseas missions that ignored needs close to home. The fear that social action would inevitably compromise the personal dimensions of the gospel and lead to theological liberalism dissipated. Even Harvard theologian Harvey Cox had to revise his widely heralded '60s prophecies of the end of personal religious faith in urban areas.[2]

A corresponding change was beginning to occur with the government's obvious failure to legislate an end to poverty through increased public spending and government-sponsored programs. Until recently, Evangelical Christians were in step with the rest of society in assuming that the government should and would provide assistance to people in need. Social ministries were opposed for diverting resources from the Church's main task, but also for intruding into activities delegated to the nation. With the reality of scarce resources, political and government leaders began to call upon the private sector to partner with the government. A move began to privatize the social service delivery system. The government began contracting with nonprofit organizations to provide a range of social programs, including low-income housing and health care. Both inside and outside of organized religion, a consensus was building that the Church bears some responsibility for solving the major problems facing society.

The first Nazarene church-sponsored social or compassionate ministry programs were hardly models for others to follow. They emerged from unique situations, with leaders who were able to attract enough funds to establish programs that could be sustained by using nondenominational resources. The network of Nazarene Compassionate Ministries in the United States and Canada now includes local congregations, with volunteer, low-cost programs, and an increasing number of church-sponsored nonprofit organizations.[3]

Although the resurgence of compassionate ministries did not wait for a clearly stated theological rationale, yet for it to be sustained in the long run, and in order to establish compassionate ministries as essential to the Christian faith, a carefully developed theology is necessary. Developing a theological rationale for compassionate ministry requires thought and planning for the structures needed to organize and direct church-sponsored social ministries. Other than directing certain volunteer relief efforts such as clothes and food distribution, most local churches are not appropriately organized to direct social service programs. As the government social service delivery system within the United States has become increasingly complex, it has become equally complicated for churches to engage themselves in direct service to people in need.

The shape of the church must be determined by its mission. Often the reverse is true. The mission of a congregation may be determined more by a building or a schedule of services, simply because this is the time of the week the congregation has always met. These reasons may have little if anything to do with creating a thoughtful strategy aimed at achieving agreed-upon mission goals and objectives. Creating appropriate organizational structures to carry out the mission of the church is in itself of theological importance. When compassionate ministry is a part of the mission of a local congregation, as well as being a priority at the denominational level, some attention must be given to creating the new and sometimes innovative structures for these ministries.

If a congregation is unclear about its mission, introducing compassionate ministry to its activities has the potential of creating conflict within the congregation. For instance, how should the finances be divided among the various needs of the congregation? Should its resources be applied to a new or renovated building or to the needs of people in the neighborhood? Establishing priorities—making decisions about the use of limited resources and about which human needs to address—are practical issues that must be decided by theological reflection that leads to action. This involves an examination of how church organizations, buildings, and budgets contribute to or detract from the church's mission.

The need for new structures for compassionate ministry (and for a theological rationale) results not only from the increasing complexity of doing compassionate ministry in a developed economy but also from the way Evangelical Protestant churches have developed in the mid-20th century. Gibson Winter, in his 1962 book *The Suburban Captivity of the Churches: An Analysis of Protestant Responsibility in the Expanding Metropolis,* described the distinct characteristics of typical 20th-century Protestant congregations.[4] Churches in middle-class suburban neighborhoods are organized to meet the needs of member families. Their mission is to provide services and programs for each member of the family, from the youngest to the seniors. While they are somewhat geographically specific, Protestant churches, unlike Catholic churches, are not primarily parish or neighborhood oriented. When a neighborhood goes through a racial change, for instance, a parish-oriented church usually remains, changing with the neighborhood. On the contrary, when a family-oriented congregation finds itself in a changing neighborhood, it usually relocates. Winter anticipated the discussions promoted by the church growth movement about "homogeneous" congregations.[5] Family-oriented churches, he observed, are usually made up of families from one racial or ethnic group and are not well suited for the pluralism of the city.

"White flight" is a commonly understood reference to congregations that relocate outside the inner cities when those areas begin to attract minorities and suffer economic deterioration. If the mission of a congregation is to serve its member families wherever they live rather than serve the neighborhood that surrounds the church building, then when its families move, the church as a body of believers has in fact already moved—regardless of the building's location. Vacating a church building in order to relocate in or near a neighborhood where surrounding families more typically resemble the member families may be entirely consistent with the mission of a family-oriented congregation.

By contrast, compassionate ministry is intentionally directed to neighborhood needs. This does not diminish the importance of ministries to families in a compassionate ministry program. However, the definition of "family" has to be flexible enough to accommodate the demographics in many needy neighborhoods. Increasingly, poor and minority families are headed by females. In the inner cities there are many single adults whose only family may be the congregation itself. The shape of the church will be affected when many, if not most, of the people in a neighborhood do not reside in nuclear families (father, mother, and children together). Then it becomes necessary to merge the "family" and "parish" church models.

At the turn of the 20th century it was common for congregations to conduct a variety of social services, including rescue missions, rest cottages (homes for unwed mothers), and orphanages.[6] This was before the time of public assistance (welfare), Medicaid, Medicare, social security, food stamps, and many other government-sponsored social programs. Engaging in 20th- and 21st-century social services will require much more thought than overlaying organizational structures from the present or past on new problems. Even a decade ago, problems such as family homelessness, "boarder babies," crack cocaine addiction, AIDS, and the unprecedented increase in street violence were unheard of. The same kind of organizational imagination that inspired Wesley in 18th-century England and Phineas Bresee at the turn of this century is needed now to create new church structures to meet the needs of people in their times.

Sometimes forgotten in this discussion is the fact that Evangelical churches, which even recently were resisting involvement in social programs at home, were at the same time generously supporting overseas missionary enterprises that included health care, education, and economic development (or social transformation). It has always been assumed that in underdeveloped economies the role, if not the mandate, of the Church is to help people overcome material and economic hardships. There is hardly anyone in the Evangelical Church more idealized than a missionary nurse or doctor. It is not surprising then that Nazarene Compassionate Ministries originated within the World Mission Division.

While Nazarene Compassionate Ministries is in its infancy in the United States, Canada, and other developed economies of Europe and Asia, relief and social transformation ministries have always played a major role in the modern missionary enterprise in undeveloped countries. Compassionate Ministries within the World Mission Division of the Church of the Nazarene employs an organizational structure through which social programs can be initiated and directed. There is no comparable delivery system in the United States and Canada. Here it is a grassroots movement in which ministries of compassion emerge from the interests within a local congregation.

Enlisting a congregation in compassionate ministries requires the creation of a clear mission statement. This includes thinking about how financial and human resources should be used and to whom the ministry of the church is directed. A thorough needs assessment should be conducted before programs are proposed and undertaken.

It has become increasingly clear that in a world where United States and Canadian cities have immigrant neighborhoods that resemble many mission fields, the distinctions between ministry at home and abroad no longer apply. Nevertheless, the motivation for compassionate ministry may be coming as much from the church's historic missionary priorities as from any other source.

⇜ PART II ⇝

Bringing Needs and Resources Together

Changing times demand new ideas and new structures. The gospel of the Kingdom requires prophetic imagination to bridge the gap separating the rich and the poor.

Compassionate ministries are organized around a simple equation: bringing needs and resources together. Whether in a local congregation or in some other organization, compassionate ministry programs stand between the needs and resources, with one hand holding on to the weak and unfortunate and the other reaching out to those called to be good stewards of the resources necessary to build the Kingdom. It is critically important to create structures that encourage and empower people.

This is precisely what John Wesley did in 18th-century England. He always professed loyalty to traditional theology and even arranged the meetings of the "classes" and "bands" so that his followers, the first Methodists, could attend worship in the Church of England on Sunday morning. What preserved the harvest of his evangelism and laid the foundation for the Wesleyan-Holiness Movement were the simple, reproducible structures in which the urban poor, to whom his ministry was directed, could be served and equipped for service to others.

There are many examples of organizations, particularly government agencies, that, while well-enough intentioned, contribute to the problems they attempt to solve. It is increasingly acknowledged that social services conducted by faith communities do a better job of helping people transform their lives.

Creating structures or organizations for compassionate ministries involves finding the "new wineskins" Jesus spoke of in Matt. 9:17. There is no lack of interest within the Church in responding to human need. While churches always struggle with limited financial resources, compassionate ministries have proven to be a magnet for funds from beyond the offering plates. Without compromising their central religious values, church-sponsored nonprofit organizations have been successful in attracting broad support from beyond the Church, including grants from corporations and foundations.

Finding "new wineskins" for compassionate ministries requires the creation of organizational structures that can bring together human needs and available resources. The local congregation and denominational leadership are essential partners in this process.

During recent years a two-tiered delivery system has developed in the United States and Canada within Nazarene Compassionate Ministries. Organized compassionate ministries usually begin within a congregation. Pastors and laypersons take it upon themselves to respond to some human need. Beginning in 1992, such congregations were recognized at Nazarene district assemblies as "Good Samaritan churches." Because they are close to the people, congregations will always be closest to human need and be the place with the biblical and theological mandates to motivate members to serve others. Local congregations will also benefit from receiving into membership those who have become followers of Jesus through compassionate ministry.

Programs that begin within a congregation often need financial support beyond the resources of the members. Given the complexity of engaging in social services, compassionate ministries often require separately incorporated nonprofit organizations to carry out their programs. Nonprofit, tax-exempt organizations can attract funds from foundations and corporations as well as from government agencies.

There has been some fear that separately incorporated nonprofits would break their ties to the local church. Experience in recent years has proven the opposite. The compassionate ministry centers, as they have been identified since 1992, have become close allies of congregations. They offer to congregations a place of volunteer service for members of churches located away from needy neighborhoods. In some instances they provide referrals to pastors and churches who need to offer advice to people in need of social services. Many times the compassionate ministry centers have contributed to significant growth within sponsoring or nearby congregations.

The rationale for compassionate ministry involves more than a need to go beyond the limitations of government social service programs. There is a significant value added to social programs when conducted by people of faith. First and foremost, people in need are offered spiritual as well as temporal help. In many different ways, the words and deeds of the gospel combine in compassionate ministry.

In addition, every needy person is seen by a faith community as a potential helper if not a leader. The line between those with needs and those with resources is removed. This contrasts sharply with government social services, in which the line separating those who need help from those who dispense it has become a wall. Most compassionate ministry programs provide opportunities for clients to participate and eventually assume places of leadership within the organization. Such respect for the worth and potential of each person comes from the basic spiritual orientation of compassionate ministries. These programs, as the congregations from which they have grown, are committed to building the Kingdom, not just to providing needed social services.

In recent years, Good Samaritan churches and compassionate ministry centers have engaged in a wide variety of programs concentrated in housing, health care, and educational programs for all ages. They can be found in the ghettos of inner cities, suburban neighborhoods, and even rural areas. Many of these ministries have restored abandoned buildings once thought useless. Empty church buildings in deteriorating neighborhoods have become round-the-clock, seven-days-a-week places of refuge and worship. Needy people—homeless, addicted, and sick—have been resurrected, bringing hope to congregations old and new.

4 ☙

Compassionate Ministry Centers

*Compassionate ministry centers provide a place to
demonstrate evangelism as both service and
proclamation. They stand between church and society,
with one hand reaching out to those in need and the
other holding on to those with resources.*

The development of compassionate ministry centers
(church-endorsed, if not church-sponsored, charitable
organizations) during the past decade is the most visible
and unprecedented result of the denomination's commitment to responding to needy people. The theological and
organizational changes creating the climate in which
these ministries have evolved could not have been imag-
ined as late as the mid-1970s. Until very recently, compassionate ministries needed an explanation if not a defense.
Now it is the reverse. Nazarenes expect the church to respond to the poor and the needy whether they are victims
of natural disaster or of chronic poverty in rural areas and
urban settings.

A few of the 85 Nazarene compassionate ministry
centers listed in 1996 in the United States and Canada pre-
date the organization of Nazarene Compassionate Ministries in the mid-1980s. (For a complete listing, see the Ap-
pendix.) The following is a glimpse into a few of these
ministry centers.

In Kansas City, home of the International Center of the
Church of the Nazarene, is the Kansas City Rescue Mission.

It was founded in 1950 by the late Jarrette Aycock, an evangelist who served as superintendent of the Kansas City District of the denomination until the mid-1960s. Rev. Aycock was himself converted in a Los Angeles rescue mission. He established and supported the Kansas City mission to provide for others like himself the opportunity to recover and begin a new life. In 1991 the mission moved into a newly renovated 100-bed facility with expanded recovery and training programs. From its beginning, the mission has enjoyed the leadership and support of Kansas City Nazarenes.

The Kansas City Rescue Mission has been led through its recent dramatic growth and relocation by Rev. Joe Colaizzi, a convert of the Lamb's ministry in the Times Square area of midtown Manhattan in New York City. Its founder, Rev. Paul Moore, became widely known in the Jesus Movement of the 1960s—with his long hair, rock music, clerical collar, and jeans. From its start in New Jersey, the ministry moved to New York, meeting in rented churches and in Central Park with outdoor Christian rock concerts. The services were exciting and controversial for the time, clearly challenging the normal ways of "doing church" in an urban setting among people who seldom if ever would be found in established churches.

The Manhattan Project, as it was then called, had the opportunity to purchase, for a fraction of its present value, the Lamb's Club. It was a deteriorating landmark built in the 19th century as a theater guild. These maverick inner-city ministers put their own interpretation on the name as well as the building. The building transformed the ministry as much as the workers did the building. The rooms and dining facilities of what was once one of New York's most exclusive clubs are now used by the Lamb's Church of the Nazarene to feed and house the city's hungry and homeless.

While it was a few years before the Lamb's Church of the Nazarene organized a separate charitable organization to develop resources for social ministries, the Lamb's was clearly a ministry designed to respond to the poor of the city. It received widespread support from people and churches across the country, most notably from Pasadena (California) First Church of the Nazarene and Pastor Earl Lee. Something new was happening. An innovative ministry combining evangelism and social action was receiving widespread attention and support from some of the denomination's most respected leaders.

The Community of Hope, located two miles directly north of the White House in Washington, D.C., was organized soon after the Lamb's center. In 1971 I came to the area to serve as the senior pastor of Washington First Church of the Nazarene. This historic congregation with a commuting, predominantly white membership was unique in that it remained in the city even as the neighborhood around the church was populated by African-Americans. As I looked around the city within walking distance of our church, it was clear that the nearby ghettos were filled with people who were unlikely ever to be reached by the church as we knew it then.

A group of First Church members formed a mission group and in cooperation with a newly formed nonprofit housing corporation—Jubilee Housing—assumed responsibility for the management and renovation of a deteriorating, overcrowded building housing 48 families—most of them on welfare. In cooperation with the Washington District, First Church began contributing to a fund to begin an inner-city mission. It was not long before I realized that my calling was to resign from my position and ask District Superintendent Carnahan to appoint me to plant a church in Washington's inner city. The Washington Inner-city Mission held its first service December 5, 1975, in the Potter's House, a coffeehouse operated by the Church of the Savior in nearby Adams Morgan, one of Washington's most ethnically diverse neighborhoods.

For two years we met for worship in the Potter's House. We spent our weekdays and evenings organizing volunteers to help rehabilitate the apartment building and respond to the needs of the people on the 1400 block of Belmont Street N.W. During the formative days of the ministry, which we would eventually name the Community of Hope Church of the Nazarene, we thought of our calling as somewhat of an experiment. We had no assurance of financial support and wondered how effectively we could combine the personal and social dimensions of the gospel. Almost to our surprise, we enjoyed widespread attention. Even more unanticipated was the support we received from the Washington District churches as well as from individuals across the country.

In 1977 the Community of Hope Church was able to purchase a building of its own on Belmont Street. This 27-unit building was uninhabitable. We boarded up the windows and began to restore the building one room at a time. Within a month we were able to renovate a first-floor apartment into a small chapel and open our doors for worship to our Belmont Street neighbors. A year later we completed the minimal repairs needed to allow people to live in some of the apartments. The building, known by its address, 1417 Belmont, became an incubator for a variety of ministries begun by committed Christians, including legal, medical, educational, and social work professionals. Even before family homelessness had become as widely recognized as it would become in the 1980s, we decided to make use of the apartments for emergency housing for homeless families.

As with the Lamb's in New York City, the purchase of 1417 Belmont was a turning point for the Community of Hope. Having a strategically located property in one of the city's most needy neighborhoods provided the opportunity to put a vision into action. It was not until 1981, however, that the congregation realized that it needed to incorporate as a separate nonprofit charitable organization in order to support its expanding ministries of housing, health care, and education. By 1990 the Community of

Hope, Inc., had an annual budget of more than $1 million. When Nazarene Compassionate Ministries was formed in 1984, our small mission congregation in the inner city was well on its way. We were demonstrating it was possible to begin replicating what Wesley and Bresee had done in their times—targeting a ministry toward the poor, responding to both their spiritual and temporal needs.

During that same time others were being called to develop ministries that would eventually be identified as compassionate ministry centers. In 1964 Gertrude Jones, a Nazarene laywoman, began a boarding school for Native American children in Sun Valley, Arizona. Known for years as Twin Wells Indian School, it was reorganized and incorporated in 1987, with Nazarene leadership, as Native American Ministries. It is identified now as the Sun Valley Indian School. The boarding school with a budget of more than $600,000 has an enrollment of 135 children aged 6-15 in grades one through eight. It has received major support from Nazarene Child Sponsorship and Work and Witness rehabilitation and construction teams.

In 1972 Monroe and JoeAnn Ballard, an African-American couple in Memphis, began to care for foster children. Monroe, an elementary school teacher, and JoeAnn, who had spent her childhood in an orphanage, opened their home and eventually purchased other homes next door and across the street from their house to provide housing and education for "adult children" aged 17 to 25. They have assisted many of these young people to attend college.

Rev. JoeAnn Ballard founded and has directed the Neighborhood Christian Center (NCC) in Memphis since its beginning in 1978. NCC has now spread to 40 sites in several Southern states, including Tennessee, Mississippi, and Georgia. Under her leadership, Neighborhood Christian Centers have received widespread support and attention for their "Christian social work" as well as tutoring and mentoring programs for at-risk children and youth.

In 1972 Rev. Gilbert Leigh, a Chicago-area Nazarene

minister, started New World Christian Ministries, an early childhood program for disadvantaged Chicago children. During the 1980s it grew into an extensive Head Start program for disadvantaged children, with a budget of $3 million. Rev. Leigh has recently organized Douglas-Tubman Youth Ministries to continue ministries to needy children and youth.

In the late 1970s Mike Christenson, on staff at the Lamb's, moved to California to begin a ministry in San Francisco's notorious Haight-Ashbury district. This area was home of the 1960s countercultural movement and more recently crowded with homeless street people. Golden Gate Compassionate Ministries purchased the Oak Street House as a home for worship and social outreach. Golden Gate was strategically located and spiritually prepared to respond to the victims of the AIDS plague that surfaced in the early 1980s. The structure for ministry was repeated—a faith community called to serve the poor and the needy, a strategic location, and a charitable organization supported by traditional churches.

Compassionate ministries were to evolve from very different circumstances at Los Angeles First Church of the Nazarene, the mother church of the denomination. Demographic changes in the 1970s and 1980s transformed the neighborhood around Los Angeles First almost overnight. An elaborate sanctuary with stained-glass windows and pipe organ, built in 1961 to serve a middle- to upper-class membership, was now surrounded by a relatively poor immigrant population from various Asian and Hispanic countries, most of whom could not speak English. The handwriting was on the wall—either adapt quickly, or see the end of a ministry founded by Phineas Bresee.

Under the direction of Dr. Ron Benefiel, a young pastor who had previously served the congregation as youth minister, the church has experienced one of the most dramatic renewals of any inner-city church. To the English-speaking congregation (which in itself is ethnically diverse) were added Filipino, Korean, and Spanish congregations, each with its own pastor, sharing space and collaborating in neighborhood ministries. The P. F. Bresee Foundation was formed as a nonprofit ministry of the church to provide a structure for charitable ministries as well as a training center for urban ministry and is now a graduate program in cooperation with Nazarene Theological Seminary.

These were some of the beginnings. By the time Nazarene Compassionate Ministries was formed in 1984, there already existed in the United States and Canada a change of attitude if not theology. A genuine grassroots movement, led by lay members as often as the clergy, was emerging. The denomination's lead in creating the Nazarene Compassionate Ministries office was matched by the growing interest of churches and church members in charitable Christian work that had always been central to the church's mission.

The historic precedent for Nazarene Compassionate Ministries is obvious in another Los Angeles ministry, but until recently it was hardly recognized for its Nazarene roots. The Los Angeles Mission, with a $15 million annual budget, has become one of the most modern and progressive gospel missions in the country. It traces its beginning to the Peniel Mission, where Phineas Bresee served in the late 1800s prior to organizing a cooperative ministry to the poor of the city—naming the new mission First Church of the Nazarene. Both the immediate past executive director, Mark Holzinger, and the present director, Mike Edwards, are Nazarene ministers. Board Chairman Dick Willis and several board members are likewise members of the Church of the Nazarene. Until the formation of Nazarene Compassionate Ministries and the identification of compassionate ministry centers, there was no way of recognizing this historic ministry as well as the newer ministries.

It's impossible in such a brief survey to do justice to all the ministries referred to as well as those not mentioned. We have realized from the beginning of Nazarene

Compassionate Ministries that there is more going on than is widely known. Each compassionate ministry center has its own story, which if fully described would each fill a book well worth reading.

Much of the motivation for the development of compassionate ministries came from two national conferences cosponsored with Nazarene Theological Seminary in 1985 and 1989. The first conference featured speakers from outside the denomination. To everyone's surprise, more people came than had registered or were planned for. It was the first time a cross section of pastors, church members and leaders, academicians and students had gathered to share their common vision for responding to the poor. A book edited by Steve Weber, director of Nazarene Compassionate Ministries since its 1984 beginning, and Al Truesdale, professor at Nazarene Theological Seminary, was published.

By the time of the second conference in 1989, so much new activity had been identified that the speakers were all from within the growing network of compassionate ministry programs. The motivation and direction for compassionate ministries was coming from within. In 1993-94, rather than one national conference, each Nazarene college/university hosted a regional conference featuring compassionate ministries from the educational zones. Following these regional conferences throughout the United States and Canada, it became clear that compassionate ministry centers were no longer simply the result of a few visionaries willing to step outside the mainstream to perform a unique ministry.

Along with an annual leadership conference for compassionate ministry center directors, the designation of these organized ministries as compassionate ministry centers was initiated in 1990. Every center must commit to being in harmony with the mission of the Church of the Nazarene by seeking to respond to the spiritual as well as the economic needs of economically disadvantaged people.

The services rendered must be nondiscriminatory. To be identified as a compassionate ministry center, the organizations must have their basic organizational documents on file with Nazarene Compassionate Ministries' United States-Canada office and submit a board resolution seeking identification with the network. With the recommendation of the District Advisory Board and district superintendent, a compassionate ministry center may become an Approved Mission Special of the Church of the Nazarene, allowing local congregations to receive credit toward their missionary giving by contributing to the ministry.

With the approval, and in some instances the direct sponsorship, of districts, compassionate ministry centers have become an accepted if not expected component of the church's mission in needy neighborhoods. The Thrust to the Cities program announced by the general superintendents during the 1985 General Assembly in Anaheim, California, committed $50,000 to each Thrust city for the support of compassionate ministries. These funds have been used for the most part as start-up grants to begin ministries, which have continued. Following the 1988 Thrust to the Cities program in Los Angeles, Rev. Mike Vasquez began Children of the Shepherd, a ministry to street people that includes runaway teens in Hollywood.

Mike and his all-volunteer staff provide weekly meals, clothing distribution, and medical assistance, along with a schedule of Bible studies and worship. From this unlikely constituency they have organized a congregation to provide a spiritual home for those served as well as those who are called to minister to young and old living in Hollywood.

Like Mike Vasquez, Scott Chamberlain made his way to Los Angeles following his graduation from Olivet Nazarene University, where he was student body president during his senior year. With the encouragement of Los Angeles First Church, he began hanging out in an inner-city park near the location where Bresee began the

Church of the Nazarene in 1895. Scott's strategy was to begin a ministry without walls. As his following increased, he organized Central City Community Outreach to provide emergency services to homeless people from the parks and after-school programs for children living in deteriorating inner-city hotels. Central City also has formed and organized a congregation from those who have been touched by compassionate ministries.

The 1992 Thrust to the Cities project in San Francisco produced two new compassionate ministry centers. The Alameda Church of the Nazarene organized New Beginning Family Services, a program to reach at-risk children and youth. While pastor of San Francisco First Church, Mike Funk began a program for youth in an often overlooked Asian neighborhood. He resigned as pastor and, with district support including a start-up grant from Nazarene Compassionate Ministries, he established the Sunset District Community Development Corporation with a primary mission to reach Asian gang members. In 1994 they received a major grant from the city and secured a property from which a variety of community development activities, youth programs, and Bible studies are conducted. Charlie Au Sing, a Chinese-American Nazarene minister, has joined the staff as a counselor and church planter.

It was the 1990 Thrust to the Cities project in Toronto that resulted in the organization of the first Canadian compassionate ministry center at the site of the old Toronto Grace Church of the Nazarene. Like inner-city churches in the United States, the Grace congregation had been declining for years. Thrust Director Marjorie Osborne led Toronto Nazarenes to organize the Sharing Place at the old church property as a multiservice agency with emergency services and counseling for Toronto's poor and needy. Soon after that, the Siloam Mission in Winnipeg was organized to provide meals and counseling for homeless people, primarily Natives who converge on the city from the Canadian prairies. The Toronto Thrust became an all-Canadian event, with support and interest generated throughout the country.

Pastor Liz Wall, on staff at Vancouver, British Columbia, First Church of the Nazarene, began to organize volunteers to respond to the needs of people in Vancouver's inner city. With strong district support, Liz organized the new compassionate ministry center, Mission Possible. In 1994 they moved into a new building, from which meals are served and rehabilitation groups and Bible studies are conducted.

The keynote speaker at the Compassionate Ministries Conference in November 1993 at Northwest Nazarene College (the first Nazarene institution to offer a major in compassionate ministries) was Jerry Ketner of Colorado Springs, founder and director of New Hope in the Rockies. Jerry, an experienced pastor and educator, persuaded a group of his friends to start a church and form a board with a ministry to the poor and needy of Colorado Springs. On Sundays, Jerry preaches to an ethnically and economically diverse congregation, many of whom have been introduced to the Lord through compassionate ministries. During the week he and a small staff organize volunteers to provide one of the city's best-known emergency services to needy residents and transients.

In 1994 New Hope in the Rockies started a second site in a Nazarene church in Pueblo, Colorado, an hour's drive south of Colorado Springs. District Superintendent Leon Wyss asked Jerry and the New Hope staff to begin a ministry in a church where an older congregation had been disorganized. They began with a full schedule of after-school activities for children and emergency services for the neighborhood. More than 100 local people attended the first service in September 1994. Through a new compassionate ministry center, needy people were served and a church was reborn.

In several instances, compassionate ministry centers have served to provide new life to older congregations in changing neighborhoods. One of the best examples is the Shepherd Community in Indianapolis. When Indianapolis First Church of the Nazarene relocated, the old property near the center of the city was left to a small, struggling core of members. In 1986 Dean Cowles and John Hay Jr. were invited as a team to provide pastoral leadership for the church and to create a nonprofit organization to provide emergency services to inner-city residents.

With significant support from First Church and Indianapolis Westside Church, as well as other district churches, Shepherd Community began an aggressive program, combining invigorating worship and evangelism along with a wide range of social services. These services include food and clothing for the homeless, a drop-in center for the elderly poor, and neighborhood housing renovation.

During the 1993 General Assembly in Indianapolis, Shepherd Community became the focal point for the highly visible infusion of Nazarene volunteerism organized by Lay Ministries under the direction of Gary Morsch. Dr. Morsch is a physician from Olathe, Kansas, who has organized Heart to Heart, an international relief organization. He correctly understood that the Indianapolis media and city leaders would appreciate and publicize a group of church conventioneers who would take time to help the poor of the city. Several hundred volunteers participated. Some of them came to the city a few days before the beginning of General Assembly to help renovate deteriorating housing near Shepherd Community. Delegates to the Nazarene Youth International Convention cleaned up city parks. Outside the convention center a large truck served as a drop-off point for General Assembly delegates, who were asked to bring nonperishable food items to be distributed through the Shepherd Community and other compassionate ministry centers.

General Assembly workers also helped renovate a recently purchased church property. In this large, vacant building with a gymnasium as well as a sanctuary and ample religious education facilities, Shepherd Community expanded its neighborhood ministry even as a new congregation was being formed. The Shepherd Community Church is now a growing congregation with expanding compassionate ministries, setting a pattern of renewal in several other inner-city churches.

Other examples of central- or inner-city churches being reorganized and revitalized around a compassionate ministry center are St. Petersburg First Church of the Nazarene and Orlando First Church of the Nazarene, on the Central Florida District. The Door of Hope was organized to conduct neighborhood ministries for needy children and families following years of decline at First Church in St. Petersburg. A nearly empty church building has now become busy again, not only on Sundays but also through the week with after-school and evening programs for neighborhood children.

More recently, the property vacated by the relocation of Orlando First Church has become the home of a new church and compassionate ministry center named Restore Orlando. Several years ago when the congregation began its relocation plans, Rev. Jerry Appleby was invited to join the staff in order to organize a ministry to the neighborhood that would remain after the relocation. They first incorporated Restore Orlando, a nonprofit compassionate ministry center, as a neighborhood ministry to needy children and youth. With district financial support, they were able to plant a new church and expand the neighborhood ministries when the First Church congregation moved.

A very different approach has been taken in Detroit. Here the district superintendent and Advisory Board took the lead in organizing Detroit Impact, a center for compassionate ministries with a ministerial training center extension of Nazarene Bible College. Located close to inner-city Nazarene churches, Detroit Impact serves both as a neighborhood youth ministry and a resource center for other congregations in needy neighborhoods. This was one of the first compassionate ministry centers with a full-time director organized by a district and supported by district churches. Since then, several districts have become actively involved in starting and supporting compassionate ministries.

One of the most aggressive district compassionate ministry programs is Common Ground Ministries in Cincinnati and Dayton, on the Southwestern Ohio District, founded and directed by Dennis Dalton. Dennis points back to a student trip to the Community of Hope in Washington, D.C., as the time when he began to contemplate his own ministry vision. On staff with the district now, Dennis has organized ministries of housing and emergency services while starting a church in Cincinnati's inner city. This ministry has also renovated several abandoned residential properties for their transitional housing program for homeless families. Common Ground provides a means of receiving contributions and grants from outside the denomination. Dennis and his small staff are now giving direction to neighborhood compassionate ministries in two inner-city churches in Dayton.

Nowhere are churches organized and assisted for service more effectively than on the New England District, through the direction of the Cambridge Institute, directed by Chris Wiley. The institute, with offices in the Cambridge (Massachusetts) First Church of the Nazarene, provides urban training curriculum for college credit as well as a variety of seminars and programs to help Boston-area churches reach needy people with the gospel.

Lay members as often as clergy are likely to find their calling to serve and/or direct compassionate ministry centers. Jim Cochenour, president of Cogan Industries, a construction firm specializing in church building, became concerned about unchurched youth in Columbiana, a small eastern Ohio town. While they were members of Columbiana First Church of the Nazarene, he and his wife, Pat, rented a storefront property on a main street and opened the Way Station, a drop-in center for youth. To get started, volunteers opened the center on weekends. Then, with Pat's social work training, other programs including alcohol and drug abuse counseling were added. Jim Cochenour has recently reduced his commitment to the construction company in order to give more of his attention to the direction of the Way Station, which, although separately incorporated, has become an effective outreach of Columbiana First Church.

Nazarene layman C. R. Smith put his furniture business on hold to follow his calling to young people in Orlando, Florida. At his own expense he acquired a storefront and opened a drop-in center for teens. Young people were attracted to the recreation and athletic activities provided. It is now called Frontline Outreach Ministries, with a variety of programs responding to the educational and vocational needs of inner-city youth offered.

In some instances, compassionate ministry centers have become the avenue through which people have heard and responded to a call to ordination. One of the most dedicated servants in the Boston area was Esther Sanger. A nurse by training, she was involved in compassionate ministry for much of her adult life and finally ordained in 1993. For Esther, ordination was the confirmation of a lifelong conviction—to have the church recognize her service as ministry worth ordination.

As the founder and director of the Quincy Crisis Center, Esther was honored for her civic and humanitarian work as a local Mother Teresa in Quincy, Massachusetts. Her home, just a few steps from Eastern Nazarene College, served as headquarters for volunteers who kept the basement stocked with the food and emergency supplies. These supplies were then distributed to the homeless and destitute in the South Boston area. She organized the Mary Martha Learning Center, a home for young homeless women either pregnant or with young children. The women live together in a sheltered retreat setting and are enrolled in various educational and vocational training programs. They are taught how to find and keep housing and jobs. The children are cared for while the mothers pursue their studies.

Esther brought with her a number of experiences remembered from her days as a foster child. She spent time in several homes herself before being introduced to a home where a Nazarene family provided the love and stability she needed.

Brother Paul, as he is identified in the book about Rev. Paul Holderfield, began his journey toward mission and ministry in the 1960s. While a fireman, Rev. Holderfield participated in hosing down civil rights demonstrators in his hometown of Little Rock, Arkansas. He eventually laid down the hoses and found a way to organize a church named Friendly Chapel, where he could welcome some of the people he had oppressed. As a self-taught minister, Paul was called to feed as well as preach to the poor.

In a pattern that has become common, the Friendly Chapel Church of the Nazarene organized a compassionate ministry center to provide a broader support base for its neighborhood ministries. Some claim that Brother Paul is the best-known preacher in Little Rock. This ex-prizefighter and former firefighter is now fighting spiritual and physical poverty. His feeding programs generate widespread local support.

The origin of these compassionate ministry centers has been the result of a real grassroots movement within the church. The organization of Nazarene Compassionate Ministries in 1984 and the establishment of a separate Nazarene Compassionate Ministries office for the United States and Canada have provided a way to draw attention to the ways people are reaching out to people in need. Within a two-year period, 1992-94, more than 20 new compassionate ministry centers were recognized. Some of them had been involved with service programs previously, but only then were they recognized.

These new compassionate ministry centers include Mercy Mission in Appalachia, a multiservice ministry sponsored by the Eastern Kentucky District and directed by Rev. Mark East; the Home for New Beginnings in Greenville, South Carolina, providing transitional housing for homeless women and children and directed by Frances Hines; Care Ministry, for the mentally and physically challenged in rural Lisbon, New Hampshire, with Lorna Safford as director; Reach Out, providing transitional housing for homeless families on Maryland's eastern shore, with Julia Parker as director; and Cunningham Christian Youth Village, a residential and educational facility for foster youth, directed by Bob and Donnell Smith in western Montana. At the time of this writing, one of the newest compassionate ministry centers is the Family Life and Counseling Center, organized at the Blue Hills Community Church of the Nazarene in Kansas City by Pastor Larry Lott and Director Sheila Harper.

Throughout the United States and Canada, these and other compassionate ministry centers are addressing some of society's most critical problems: hunger, homelessness, unemployment, and at-risk children and youth. Even the AIDS epidemic has prompted a response. In 1988 Nazarene Compassionate Ministries sponsored an AIDS conference hosted by the Metro New York District. A video was produced that became one of the first of its kind among Evangelical Christians.

Several compassionate ministry centers, including Golden Gate in San Francisco and the Community of Hope in Washington, D.C., have programs directed to those with AIDS. The Christian Counseling Center in Nashville, under the direction of Michael Malloy, led the way to provide counseling services to AIDS victims and their families. Compassionate Heart, a newly organized congregation and compassionate ministry center in Kansas City, in the Westport area, is specifically targeting its ministry to the AIDS community.

For the past several years I've had the privilege of seeing most of these compassionate ministry centers, knowing their directors, and watching their volunteers and staff serve needy people at considerable sacrifice. Some have wondered if this interest in reaching out is just another fad. We're living through a time of scarce resources when we hear of "compassion fatigue," a giving up on helping others.

In 1994 I read Anna Quindlen's last column for the *New York Times*. She gave thanks for the opportunity to be a reporter for one of the world's greatest newspapers and wrote that she had waited until this moment to write this column about "Everyday Angels," a tribute to people whom she had observed who have reached out to needy people. She mentioned several of them, local caregivers known primarily in the New York area. She wrote: "I've been here, in this space, considering the great issues of the day. But the great issues, at base, are the same as they were when John the Baptist said, 'He that has two coats, let him give one to him that has none.'" She went on to say that it was the simple goodness of people who spent their lives helping the weak and unfortunate that kept her from becoming cynical over the daily news of human evil and suffering.

And so it is in these compassionate ministry centers where the great issues of the day are being addressed. Ms. Quindlen saw it correctly when she wrote that in these places of service, "Life will be hard, politics will be mean, money will be scarce, bluster will be plentiful. Yet somehow good will be done."

In the Church of the Nazarene, we know that it is where the church meets human need that the life and teachings of Jesus become real. Here the gospel becomes good news. We are learning more about what John Wesley meant when he said that he felt closest to New Testament Christianity when he stayed at the Foundry, a London home organized by his followers for indigent widows.

5

The Growing Nazarene Compassionate Ministries Network: Good Samaritan Churches, Youth Ministries, Nazarene Disaster Response

Young and old alike want to be involved in solving the critical issues facing society. People expect the Church to be there when needs are present and disaster strikes.

The increasing number of Nazarene congregations involved in some organized form of service to the poor is a sign that responding to human need has become an accepted expression of the church's mission. When compassionate ministry centers were first identified in 1992, many congregations had already developed local compassionate ministry programs directed by volunteers and financed by donations from members. They were identified as Good Samaritan churches by Nazarene Compassionate Ministries' United States-Canada office. Beginning in 1991, their pastors were presented certificates of recognition at district assemblies.

Nearly 400 Good Samaritan churches were recognized in the 1995 assemblies. They included large churches such as Bethany, Oklahoma, First Church; Pasadena,

California, First Church; and Olathe, Kansas, College Church; as well as small inner-city and rural mission congregations. These churches respond to a variety of needs in their communities.

Members of Bethany First Church are recruited to serve in a local shelter for homeless families. During the Christmas season they contribute gift certificates and other gifts for the poor, placed on or under the "angel tree," a increasingly popular national program. Bethany First Nazarene Church may be the first congregation with a staff member whose job description includes directing compassionate ministries.

Through Helping Hands, Pasadena First Church has an extensive network of volunteers ready to respond to needy neighbors. They were actively involved in disaster assistance following the January 1994 Los Angeles earthquake. This is the first known Nazarene congregation to have identified a "parish nurse," a nursing specialty beginning to attract the interest of medical professionals as well as churches, where people, particularly the older population, are looking for health care alternatives.

For several years, College Church in Olathe, Kansas, has contributed more than any other congregation to Nazarene Compassionate Ministries. In addition to generous financial support, the congregation has provided volunteers and contributions of food and clothing to the Kansas City Rescue Mission and other ministries throughout the country. College Church Pastor J. K. Warrick, while pastor of Indianapolis Westside Church, led the congregation to generous financial and volunteer support for the inner-city ministries at Shepherd Community. He wrote and spoke of the "pent-up need in the heart of believers to give." As his congregation was generous and compassionate with needy people in their own city, they increased their giving for other church appeals, too, including those to world missions.

Many affluent suburban congregations have become

Good Samaritan churches partnering with churches in needy neighborhoods. With such support, many Nazarene congregations are finding new life as they discover opportunities for ministry in low-income neighborhoods, including rural areas, small towns, and inner-city ghettos.

This grassroots compassionate ministry movement has reversed a trend. From shortly after World War II, in the early 1950s, congregations of nearly every denomination began to relocate out of inner or center cities. Their members were moving to suburban neighborhoods to escape urban poverty as well as minority and immigrant populations. The Church of the Nazarene experienced the same phenomenon. Until recently, congested inner-city neighborhoods were hardly viewed as likely places to plant new churches. Few of those training for ministry were interested in inner-city or compassionate ministry as a career.

Now much of that has changed. More often than not, when neighborhoods change, strategies are developed to sustain the congregations, with leaders and members reflecting the neighborhood. The Metro New York District, the most urban United States Nazarene district, has experienced the greatest growth of all districts, with 50 new congregations in the 10 years since the mid-1980s. District Superintendent Dallas Mucci has made a concerted effort to plant new churches in ethnically and economically diverse neighborhoods.

The Thrust to the Cities has had much to do with this change. The Thrust projects challenged what some have described as an antiurban bias in American society. By deliberately planting churches and developing compassionate ministry projects in the cities, the church placed its resources in the center of society's greatest needs, challenges, and opportunities. As a result of the Thrust to the Cities plan announced by the Board of General Superintendents during the 1985 General Assembly in Anaheim, California, new urban congregations have been started. Many of them are now recognized as Good Samaritan churches, actively involved in responding to needy people.

Rather than retreating from the cities, now the reverse is happening. Nearly every district with an urban, ethnic, or poor population has taken steps to develop its own strategic plan for ministry in these neighborhoods. In the early 1990s, cities such as Baltimore, Pittsburgh, and Oakland initiated their own version of Thrust projects, mobilizing local and regional resources to expand ministries in unlikely places. Church buildings that in the recent past were considered a liability are now considered valuable resources.

Most Good Samaritan churches serving needy people begin compassionate ministries with emergency relief programs, typically distributing food and clothing. Many churches have become involved in food distribution by receiving commodities from the United States government, particularly surplus items from the Department of Agriculture and supplies for emergencies from FEMA (Federal Emergency Management Agency). Unlike many government programs that deny funding to religious organizations, these food programs are generally available to churches.

Community food banks are another major source of food for distribution or use in feeding programs. Nearly every city and many smaller towns now have food bank warehouses, nonprofit organizations offering wholesalers tax deductions for their contributions of surplus food and household items typically found in supermarkets. Food banks make the supplies available to charitable organizations, including churches, charging by the pound. The only restriction is that the food may not be resold and must be distributed to low-income people or used to prepare meals for the poor. With these resources many congregations have built extensive storage facilities, including refrigeration units, to provide neighborhood food distribution and meal preparation.

Earnest and Jean Scheckell, members of the Church of the Nazarene in Stuart, Florida, have promoted an unusual and effective food preparation ministry. They prefer to be recognized as "compassionate evangelists." During the 1993 General Assembly in Indianapolis, they had a booth stacked with nonperishable canned food items with pictures describing their unique ministry.

The Scheckells are aware that many needy people do not know how to cook from basics, often the kind of surplus food items made available from government sources as well as the food banks. They also know that in poverty-stricken neighborhoods many people have inadequate cooking and refrigeration facilities. Food is available, but needy people often don't know how to take advantage of the resources. The Scheckells teach churches how to get and distribute surplus food and then teach people how to cook nutritious meals with Crock-Pot recipes. They travel in their recreational vehicle, offering themselves as compassionate evangelists. They conduct revival services in local churches and teach people how to care and how to cook healthful meals. They demonstrate to local churches how to reach needy neighbors through self-help compassion evangelism.

The growing interest of youth ministry groups in service projects has added enthusiasm and resources for compassionate ministries. Youth teams from churches as well as from Nazarene campus ministries have covered the country, working alongside compassionate ministry centers and Good Samaritan churches. During the last decade many youth activities have been organized to serve others, a dramatic shift from the days when the primary emphasis of youth ministries was either social activities or musical presentations. In each of its quadrennial youth gatherings Nazarene Youth International has taken the lead, organizing several thousand teen delegates in community development service projects. Each Nazarene

Youth Congress provides training for service along with discipleship studies.

The interest of young people for compassionate ministry comes as no surprise to those who have been associated with Nazarene higher education for the past generation. Before it was a noticeable trend in the churches, campus life nurtured an awareness of and a sensitivity toward those in need. The academic setting provides an opportunity for professors and students alike to reflect on the mission of the church.

In 1975, just after announcing my decision to begin an inner-city mission in Washington, D.C., I was asked to speak on a Youth in Mission tour, visiting each Nazarene college campus. The call to urban ministry seemed to catch the imagination of students everywhere. More students offered to serve than we could have possibly used. Some of them had to be persuaded to stay in school to prepare well for ministry that to them, at that time, seemed more urgent than a college education. That interest has not let up. There are still not enough compassionate ministry service opportunities for the young people who want to serve.

This youthful enthusiasm and idealism has been nurtured into well-organized campus ministries, denominationally sponsored service projects around the world, and training programs for those professing a call for a career in compassionate ministries. Each Nazarene campus now has a compassionate ministries liaison, assigned to communicate with the Nazarene Compassionate Ministries office and other campus coordinators. College conferences and courses are regularly offered to provide information and training.

The most widespread and consistent compassionate response from churches continues to be to the victims of natural disasters. This follows the pattern begun with the origin of the Hunger and Disaster Fund—whose name was changed to Nazarene Compassionate Ministries Fund only recently to reflect the broader scope of ministries to economically disadvantaged people. Appeals to assist victims of Hurricane Andrew, the August 1992 storm that devastated south Florida and southern Louisiana, produced the largest single offering for a natural disaster in the history of compassionate ministries. More than $300,000 was contributed through the general treasurer's office at the Nazarene International Center. It is likely that an equal amount was sent directly to churches and church members.

In addition to financial contributions, scores of work teams and individual volunteers offered their assistance. In some instances, volunteers just showed up at disaster sites looking for ways to help. Truckloads of building materials, nonperishable food, and household supplies filled church buildings and parking lots. The six Nazarene congregations in the Dade County, Florida, area became centers for neighborhood outreach. As a result of extensive media attention, a dedicated phone line was established just to provide information about needs and to respond to offers of service.

That disaster relief effort, organized primarily with the South Florida District and local churches, revealed the need for a church-sponsored disaster mitigation agency. This agency could effectively take advantage of the resources made available and could respond effectively to Nazarenes and their neighbors. The newly formed Nazarene Compassionate Ministries provided the organizational structure needed.

Nazarene Compassionate Ministries, Inc., was approved by the General Board during its 1991 meeting. It provides an organizational structure to attract nondenominational funds and to assist in the worldwide network of Nazarene Compassionate Ministries. It has a board of directors nominated by the Board of General Superintendents and elected annually by the General Board. It is a church-sponsored charity similar, in spirit at least, to other denominational groups such as Catholic Charities and

Lutheran Social Services. Among other things, Nazarene Compassionate Ministries has provided a way to receive USAID ocean freight reimbursement payments to defray the cost of shipping supplies to world mission areas. Federal employees may designate their annual CFC (Combined Federal Campaign) workplace contributions to Nazarene Compassionate Ministries.

Nazarene Disaster Response (NDR) was organized as a project of Nazarene Compassionate Ministries immediately following Hurricane Andrew. Disaster planning manuals were prepared, with regional and district NDR directors appointed in 1993, just in time to respond to the 1993 summer Midwest floods. This NDR response organized relief efforts in four states on six Nazarene districts. Again people gave money, sent supplies, and volunteered to help. Churches and their members expected the church to respond.

With NDR volunteers, a disaster response network is in place, providing long-range planning and preparedness in cooperation with other government and volunteer agencies. While Nazarene Compassionate Ministries projects in the United States and Canada now include a wide range of relief and development projects, the motivation for giving and serving remains the same.

Added to the idealism of its youthful members, the Church of the Nazarene itself is young enough to have members who are no more than a generation removed from the founders, who were unapologetic about their commitment to challenge economic injustice and help people in need. Nazarene Compassionate Ministries began and is nurtured in the hearts of Nazarenes who understand the biblical mandate to respond directly where people suffer from hunger and are devastated by natural disasters. Not only do Nazarenes take the Bible seriously, but also they generally agree that John Wesley and Phineas Bresee remain examples of Christian compassion to be emulated in the Church today.

The respect within the Wesleyan-Holiness Movement for biblical authority has led to a greater concern for behavioral and ethical matters than for issues of inerrancy and dispensationalism, which are more common to Fundamentalism. There is an enduring commitment within Holiness churches to recognize sin as systemic as well as personal. Compassionate ministry finds a welcome environment among believers who understand that Christian behavior is reflected in responsible social action just as it is in personal piety.

Sanctification, the central theme of Nazarenes, is optimistic about the possibilities of change, both for individuals and society. Embedded in churches of this historical and theological tradition is a belief that forgiven believers can be transformed. Without being utopian about it, this optimism influences attitudes about society. The Holiness people have never been known to withdraw. They will continue to reach out to help others. As I was informed by a participant in a seminar, "We were doing this long before it was called 'compassionate ministries.'" The recent encouragement and coordination of programs and resources provided by Nazarene Compassionate Ministries is built on this tradition, giving shape to a movement that has a life of its own.

6

New Dimensions in International Compassionate Ministries

Nazarene missions have grown rapidly where human need is most desperate. Compassionate ministries take care of the family and open doors to new fields of service.

Nazarene Compassionate Ministries funds have been and continue to be used primarily in the third world or developing countries where Nazarene missions have flourished during the past 20 years. Twenty percent of the Nazarene Compassionate Ministries Fund (formerly the Hunger and Disaster Fund) is set aside for ministries in the United States and Canada. The fund and its activities were directed by the World Mission Division until 1990, when the Nazarene Compassionate Ministries' United States-Canada office was established within the Church Growth Division. With the support of the Nazarene World Mission Society more than $3 million is being contributed annually to the Nazarene Compassionate Ministries Fund.

While there are many events and people involved, the development of Nazarene Compassionate Ministries is the result of the leadership provided from within the World Mission Division by Steve Weber. Dr. Weber is an economics graduate of California State University at Long Beach, with degrees from Nazarene Theological Seminary, California Graduate School of Theology, and Fuller Theological

Seminary. He was a missionary in Haiti from 1974 to 1984, a period when Haiti was one of the fastest-growing mission fields in the church. As mission director he was responsible for the development of a number of relief and development programs. These became prototypes for much of what Nazarene Compassionate Ministries would eventually become in the underdeveloped world where Nazarene missions have thrived in the final decades of the 20th century.

This story is told in part in four books from Nazarene Publishing House that Steve has written, coauthored, or edited: *Evangelism and Social Redemption: Addresses from the 1985 Compassionate Ministries Conference* (1986); *The Greening: The Story of Nazarene Compassionate Ministries* (1986); *The Crisis: How the Hunger and Disaster Fund Is Helping* (1987); *Saint in Overalls: The Charles Morrow Story* (1991).[1] Even the reading of these books doesn't tell the whole story and in fact may not reveal some of the significant trends that have accompanied Dr. Weber's leadership during the past 10 years.

The following dialogue with Dr. Weber was originally intended to provide research to describe the growth of compassionate ministries among the poor and needy around the world. The interview covered more than I had anticipated. Major changes have occurred in the way we think of and conduct missionary activity. Not that compassionate ministries have caused the changes—in fact, it may be the reverse. These changes, some of them not always recognized, have provided the climate in which Nazarene Compassionate Ministries is possible if not necessary.

Missionary work from the beginning of the 20th century was traditionally built around preaching, teaching, and healing. Nazarene schools and hospitals were supported and promoted as integral parts of the missionary enterprise in what were understood by the sending churches as backward countries without educational or health care systems. Missionary doctors and nurses were once as revered and idolized as the missionary preachers.

Schools and hospitals supported by missionaries came to be referred to as "institutional missions" to distinguish them from the mainline missionary work of evangelism and church planting.

Soon after midcentury, the financial demands of educational and medical institutions began to be seen as draining support from the primary evangelistic objective of missions. Furthermore, there was little evidence that committing missionary personnel to staffing schools and hospitals furthered the goal of multiplying converts and building indigenous churches. Some of the fastest-growing missions were in countries without expensive missionary-staffed institutions. Mission strategy changed. Committing limited budget funds to costly educational and medical institutions was seen as unaffordable if not a distraction from pure missionary work.

It would be wrong, however, to assume from this that there was no longer a concern on the part of the sending church or the emerging national churches for the temporal needs of destitute people who comprise the vast majority of the underdeveloped world where missions have been most successful. In my discussion with Dr. Weber, I discovered some events and trends that might be too recent for objective historical evaluation. Major changes have occurred and are occurring that transform the way we define and think about missionary activity. The most obvious is that missions are increasingly urban. Very few missionaries are sent to scarcely populated jungles without the benefit of written communication. Missionary work is now concentrated in crowded world-class cities that have all become somewhat alike in their diversity, congestion, and sharp contrasts between wealth and poverty.

In addition, the artificial distinction between evangelism and compassion has never been drawn in the developing countries where missions have thrived, and now in the Eastern bloc, recently opened to the Church. Wherever it exists and intends to establish itself, the Church is expected to respond to the quality-of-life issues that are first and foremost in most of the world, where finding the critical minimums of life is a daily struggle. While compassionate ministries may be seen as an option in the developed countries of North America, Western Europe, and Asia, in the rest of the world caring for the needy is an unavoidable mandate for Christian missions.

In my discussion with Dr. Weber, I was made aware that Nazarene Compassionate Ministries plays two key roles in the missionary enterprise. First, most compassionate ministry funds and projects are used to relieve suffering, destitution, and death among Nazarenes. Nazarene Compassionate Ministries is generally not involved in economic development projects directed to the general population. Although in cooperation with development agencies, most of the activities are directed to the expanding population of Nazarenes in these destitute areas.

Nazarene Compassionate Ministries is first and foremost a response to destitute, suffering Nazarenes. It is sobering, if not shocking, to realize that people of our own faith tradition are so much in need. The annual average income is less than $400 in Haiti and Nicaragua, the two poorest countries of the Western Hemisphere. Throughout Central America, South America, Africa, and Asia, Nazarenes are among those who suffer from lack of food, shelter, and health care. While others are not denied assistance, Nazarene Compassionate Ministries with its limited funds cannot presume to solve the problems of any one nation, let alone the world. But it can make a difference within its own fellowship. Most international and national development programs are recognizing that the most effective use of development assistance is through such structured and grassroots organizations.

The second new development coming within the 1990s is the opening of new countries for missions through Nazarene Compassionate Ministries. In the Eastern bloc particularly, but also in other world areas such as Vietnam, the Church is not permitted to enter with a traditional missionary enterprise of direct evangelism and church planting. The only opening is through some development project, when the Church brings resources to help build the economy and relieve suffering. It is through offerings to the Nazarene Compassionate Ministries Fund and the projects directed by Nazarene Compassionate Ministries that more than a dozen new countries have missions as are now described as compassion evangelism.

Responding to needy Nazarenes, including their neighbors, and leading the way in previously closed countries have become the dual mandate of Nazarene Compassionate Ministries International. It is not that different from Nazarene Compassionate Ministries in the United States and Canada, where the first concern continues to be the needs of those within the household of faith, and where previously abandoned cities are being reentered through compassionate ministries.

How these trends and events have unfolded is the subject of a discussion I had with Dr. Weber in January 1995. My comments and questions are in boldface.

When Nazarene Compassionate Ministries was started in 1984, the Hunger and Disaster Fund had been around since the mid-1970s. The fund was to provide for relief during a time of retrenchment from institutional missions.

Exactly. At one point we had several hospitals. It's hard to differentiate between what was a hospital and what was a major clinic. For example, in Haiti there was a time when we had some beds in a clinic and were delivering babies. The transition from a clinic to a hospital on the mission field is somewhat nebulous. In the mid-1970s we had four hospitals—two in Africa, one in Papua New Guinea, and one in India. In 1995 we're down to just the one in Papua New Guinea that's staffed by missionaries.

What was the origin of the Hunger and Disaster Fund?

It came out of the Haiti famine in 1974. It was the result of a telephone call I made to Dr. Jerald Johnson, who at the time was the executive secretary of the Department of World Missions. I asked for funds to respond to a famine that was killing Nazarenes. They were dying of starvation.

When Dr. Johnson sent a check for $25,000, the news was then spread around that Nazarenes were dying of hunger. What we call "Approved Specials" were coming in, marked "Haiti Hunger" or "Haiti Starvation." This wasn't the first time that happened. The difference in 1974 was that the offerings came in very big and consistently. World Missions took all those contributions and put them together in a special fund, initially called the "Hunger Fund."

Then there was the 1976 Guatemala earthquake. In northern Guatemala, Nazarenes are as thick as anywhere on the face of the earth. The earthquake hit right in the middle of us—churches, schools, parsonages. There was a flurry of what we now call "Work and Witness teams" going there, rebuilding buildings. As a result of the earthquake, the word "Disaster" was added to this Approved Special, renaming it the "Hunger and Disaster Fund."

Those disasters and others came and went. By 1983 there was $50,000 to $60,000 a month coming into that fund—nearly $500,000 during that calendar year—and no one knew why. More important, what should we do with it? The obvious solution: bring in an administrator to oversee it.

While Nazarene Compassionate Ministries had its origins in the Hunger and Disaster Fund at a time when there was a retrenchment from institutional missions, it was also a time of spontaneous heartfelt responses to victims of natural disasters.

I remember rebuilding a church in Mexico City that had been destroyed in a fire. We were proud that we had rebuilt the church with Hunger and Disaster funds—took a picture for an article in the Herald of Holiness—*and got significant negative reaction from the donors. The donors were saying, "We're sending this money to help people, to feed them; we have other programs to help build church buildings."*

It's interesting in the financing of institutional missions—the four hospitals, for instance—that while the cost became prohibitive, people still wanted to give to meet temporal needs. Two things were going on: financial priorities dictated how budgeted funds were to be used, but along with that, you also had the grassroots interest. In spite of the retrenchment from institutional missions, there was this latent interest in the temporal condition of destitute people.

You could write a book on the statement I'm about to make. In the '60s, Nazarene college students, in my opinion, wanted to be more activist than the climate on those Nazarene campuses allowed. I was a student at a secular university during the early '60s. I'm talking about my own age-group now. But the practical outworking of the desire to be involved in social issues, however you want to say that, was a group of Nazarene college graduates who became preachers and lay leaders in the early '70s. They responded, and these are provable numbers, with millions of dollars, because parachurch organizations track by denomination.

By 1984 the Nazarene sentiment was "Let's get our money back; let's offer an alternative to our own people who are giving outside our structure"—not only outside the General Budget structure, but outside the structure, period. The people didn't seem to care much about whether or not the money went through Kansas City.

Part of my instruction was to appeal to those donors. In the 1980s I was talking to people my own age, in their late 30s, early 40s, who had come through our colleges in the 1960s and were demanding that we do this. In this first year we received more than a million dollars.

What was the first thing you did when you came to the office?

One of the first, most significant things was to write thank-you letters to the people who were sending the money. That had never been done. As simple as that sounds, for 10 years people had been sending their money, and nobody had ever thanked them. Talk about denominational loyalty—how long would you send money if you never knew what happened to it? So we started immediately writing thank-you letters—not appeal letters—just a thank-you letter for $10 or $1,000, and then told them what we were doing with the money. That created a multiplier. Once they got the thank-you letter, they sent in more money, and then they got another thank-you letter.

The other thing—with the two volunteers who came with me to start the Nazarene Compassionate Ministries office, we traveled this nation. Night after night after night we traversed the land with this message: you have an option. We didn't bad-mouth the other agencies, but we simply said that Nazarenes now can give to help hungry people or sponsor a child, perhaps a pastor's child. We were offering alternatives, something the other agencies were not doing, or would never do. So we asked, "Would you like to sponsor a Nazarene pastor's child?"

Because of my knowledge of what was going on on the other side (the mission fields), I tried very hard to promote those needs, maybe as they'd never been promoted before. I encouraged missionaries—who, like me, had done this kind of work on the field—to talk about it. For example, what we now call development or social transformation projects, I encouraged the missionaries on furlough to begin talking about—such things as feeding the hungry and digging a water well to provide pure water in the village.

Things they were already doing.

But they had not been talked about in deputation services—at least in recent years. As the missionaries shared these stories, the constituency caught on.

You were promoting this fund—connected to the "two-thirds" world, as you call it—with a missionary

structure that had been moving away from institutional forms of missions. What did the Nazarene missionary enterprise outside of North America think of this new movement of compassionate ministries? What's their response or reaction to it?

Let me insert a missing link—another dimension. In the early years we didn't spend as much time working with our missionaries as with the maturing national leadership. That fact is so important. The reason we had so much receptivity on the mission field was because there were thousands of Nazarene indigenous church leaders who were excited by this new partnership.

An example is found in Mozambique. For the first two years (1985-86) of Nazarene Compassionate Ministries there were no missionaries in Mozambique. There was a war going on. The Nazarene Compassionate Ministries staff from Kansas City were the first ones there, working with the national leadership during the revolution.

In Nicaragua I had to get a special passport, because it was illegal for American citizens to go in under the Marxist president, Daniel Ortega. We were working with the national leadership.

I've heard you talk about the inevitable evolution of relief ministries to social transformation ministries. What do you mean by that?

If you view the world through sociological eyes, then you're going to name a lot of things, such as educational improvement. If you view the world through economic eyes, as I do, then the list is different. The bottom line is income generation. If you want to feed a kid, get his or her dad a job. These are the kinds of things that permeated those early years. We weren't interested in feeding programs. We were interested in income generation and vocational training—anything that would expand the income pie so that families could sustain themselves and feed their own children. Sustainability became the issue. Therefore, agriculture is more important than feeding. Growing your own food is more important than giving food away. Training someone how to do a job and providing the tools to do it became more important than a welfare giveaway program. There's something more important than teaching a person how to fish—that is how to gain access to the river. That's the justice part. It moves from relief to development to justice.

I remember visiting with you during a 1980 trip to Haiti while you were the director of missions there. You said then that your problem was not making converts or building churches, but what to do with the destitute converts who had joined the church.

These are the social consequences of doing missions in a culture that has no social support system. If a widow gets converted in Haiti and comes into the church, she brings her kids with her. The church has the responsibility not only for the woman but also for the children.

It is evidently relatively easy to make converts in these underdeveloped countries and relatively easy to build churches, including the buildings. Work and Witness teams can build a structure in two or three weeks—unheard of in this country. Traditionally, compassionate ministries enters the picture after traditional missions have been in place, and you have converts—after you've built your churches.

The United States constituency has to understand what nurturing the Body means. We're not talking about a Wednesday night Bible study. We're talking about a woman with five children who has been cut off from any economic connections. Here's a pastor looking at this woman with five children and who desperately wants her to receive Christ as Savior. That pastor knows that if he presents the gospel to her, he becomes personally responsible for her welfare and her five children. Therefore, alongside a Nazarene church in Haiti there will be a series of Quonset huts, lean-tos, along the side of the road.

Batey writes in his book *Jesus and the Poor* that the

first Christians did not set out to solve the poverty problem of the Roman Empire, but that they did solve the poverty problem in their own faith communities.

Out there in the two-thirds world, it's definitely "us" first, in the sense that they have these incredible problems among themselves.

Compassionate ministries follows Paul's example of collecting an offering from the Greeks for the impoverished believers in Jerusalem. The growth of missions has produced large numbers of Nazarenes around the world in very destitute situations.

Yet what did I preach about when I went to Mozambique, Nicaragua, or India—how poor they were and how happy I was to be Santa Claus? No—about their need to respond to people less fortunate than they were. And that needs to be understood. Those people many times give more sacrificially than we do—my point being that they too can get ingrown and pulled inward if they worry too much about themselves, and we can add to that problem by giving relief.

One of the early things that stands out in my mind happened in the 1985 General Assembly in Anaheim. I arranged a meeting between the delegation from Japan and the delegation from Mozambique. We had a luncheon when the Japanese officially handed their gift to the delegation from Mozambique. To see what that did to the Japanese delegation was a very New Testament experience. In 1994 the church in Germany handed us a $22,000 check for the Nazarenes in Rwanda. No one asked them to do that.

Nazarene Compassionate Ministries then attempts first to be sure that Nazarenes are cared for.

We have all these programs now for medical help. We have a program that attempts to guarantee that no Nazarene in the third world will die from the lack of adequate health care.

So you've got this declining interest in institutional missions, not because people are less interested in supporting medical missions, but because of the inability of the church to bear the cost within the priorities of missions.

The spontaneous, unsolicited giving to the Hunger and Disaster Fund was a signal. There's something here that we didn't anticipate and really don't know how to manage. Compassionate ministries didn't come out of a strategic plan, but out of a need to manage a significant amount of money that was coming in for reasons we may never understand precisely.

While the original missionary emphasis was to destitute people, like in the jungles of Africa, there was a notion that all we have to do is share the gospel. However, they understood in the beginning that a part of the gospel presentation was teaching and healing.

All that changed in the 1940s. We started OK from around 1908 up to and through the 1930s, but then the institutions began to sap our resources. We didn't have money to send new missionaries.

Wasn't Haiti an example of a very successful missionary enterprise without institutions?

Nothing could be farther from the truth. The reason Haiti grew so well was its school system. We had 300 schools.

But it was a different model. The schools were sustained by the local churches, the nationals rather than missionaries. Just as in the United States, people in these third world countries, too, were looking at the needs in their neighborhoods and were doing what any of us would do. After 10 years, the primary use of Nazarene Compassionate Ministries funds is for income-generation projects.

The bulk of the resources now is going to vocational training and the development of people. We've funded more than 300 microenterprise projects, including small business start-ups and agricultural programs. The second area is education, including adult nonformal education vocational training and more traditional primary education for children. The third category is health-care, community-based clinics.

We're probably not going to have more hospitals, are we?

Well, oddly enough, we have more hospitals than ever, not in the first-world concept or even in the missionary definition, but in the third world definition. If a hospital is a place where sick people come and get in a bed and stay there and are cared for, then yes.

But we're not sending out missionary doctors.

That's right—it's national workers.

That's illustrated by the 1994 conference in Quito, Ecuador, for Nazarene Compassionate Ministries leaders from Central and South America, which I attended. Of the 50 Nazarene Compassionate Ministries leaders, most of them professionals from 15 countries, 9 were medical doctors directing some medical program with the support of Nazarene Compassionate Ministries.

The last time I was there, there were 34 Nazarene medical doctors in Nicaragua alone—just one little country. It would take a chapter in your book to explain what we mean by that, because it doesn't work the same as in the United States. Many of these are government clinics operated by Nazarenes. Others are private clinics. The point is, we're funding them, supporting a nationally operated, community-based health care delivery system. There are no missionaries involved.

Other major areas of Nazarene Compassionate Ministries' international activity include refuge and disaster relief. We've not left out those things.

Compassionate Ministries now is primarily committed to helping destitute Nazarenes who will never get health care, who will never get an education, unless they get it within our system.

I could take you to churches where the congregations

do not have clothes, where Nazarene children and pastors' children still die from the lack of basic health care.

The question now is, for instance, "What is happening to the Nazarenes in Rwanda?"—not just "What is happening in Rwanda?" We can be effective only in areas where we have a base. As we've said earlier, we're not trying to solve all the poverty or destitution of the world. But we *can* make an impact. The recent earthquake in India has given us the opportunity to establish a base in that country.

That's compassion evangelism. In the last five years, since the Berlin Wall came down in November 1989, that has been the largest single thing we've done. We have entered new countries with these Nazarene Compassionate Ministries dollars—16 of them, including Cambodia, Vietnam, Romania, Bulgaria, Russia, the Ukraine, Armenia, Eritrea, Ethiopia. These were all entered with compassionate ministries money. When we say the Church of the Nazarene is in these countries, most people think of traditional missions. We're there, but we can do only compassionate ministries. We don't yet have organized churches and church members in several of those countries. But we will.

I don't think this dimension of compassionate ministries has been widely known. The theme of compassion as a lifestyle has come through, but the more pointed direction of Nazarene Compassionate Ministries has not been understood.

These two issues: opening new work and ministering to the family, the Rwandans, for instance. Those are the dual tracks, the main thrusts that we should be sharing. Compassion evangelism, entering new places, and caring for our own: that's where we are. That's the future.

CONCLUSION

During the early '80s I was invited to speak at a seminar on urban ministries as part of the events surrounding the annual National Prayer Breakfast. During the first week of every February the Fellowship Foundation invites about 2,000 people to attend this event at the Washington Hilton Hotel. The president of the United States always attends and speaks. On a couple of occasions I attended (thanks to complimentary tickets), so I was anxious for the opportunity to participate.

For the most part, the only way to attend this event is by recommendation from a member of Congress. People come from all parts of the country, anxious to pay the $100 plus for the breakfast and the privilege of listening to the president speak and seeing congressional leaders and other Washington luminaries set aside partisan politics for this annual display of public piety.

The seminar was one of many scheduled to immediately follow the breakfast. I decided to walk the mile from the Community of Hope at 14th and Belmont Streets Northwest to the Washington Hilton near 19th and Connecticut. Rather than attend the breakfast, I walked down 14th Street to Big Willies, a short-order carry-out frequented for the most part by the poorer residents of our neighborhood. My seminar objective was to describe ministry in the inner city for those attending the breakfast at the Hilton with the president. So that the contrast would be fresh in my mind, I had my coffee in a Styrofoam cup while I stood at the counter eating my doughnut, crowded into a steamy inner-city restaurant a world apart from the Hilton breakfast less than a mile away.

I began the seminar by describing what I saw that

morning and the people I knew and ministered with on a daily basis. I wanted them to know what life and ministry was like among the poor of the city, among people who never in their lives could expect to eat at the Hilton and for whom the price of that breakfast was a week's pay.

In the course of my presentation a man stood up from near the middle of the group of several hundred, challenging something I had said. It was the first time in all my years of preaching I had ever had someone interrupt me in the middle of a message. When I said, "Accumulated and hoarded wealth in the presence of human need is a moral evil," he jumped to his feet and shouted, "Where do you find that in the Bible?"

It was a statement with truth I had assumed from my reading of the Bible and was hardly prepared to defend at that moment. The only biblical reference I could recall was Luke 16:19-31, where Jesus tells the story of the afterlife of poor Lazarus and the rich man. Lazarus goes to the bosom of Abraham, while the rich man cries out from Hades that others be warned not to follow in his steps. The only reason given for the rich man's torment was his unwillingness to share his wealth with the poor man he saw daily at the gates to his mansion (v. 20).

One story doesn't make a theology, and I'm sure I didn't answer the question to the man's satisfaction. The question was not from an agnostic challenging the Christian faith. After all, he had spent a lot of money and probably traveled a long way to attend this prayer breakfast. At that moment he was deeply troubled, as we all are when we begin to take seriously our Christian responsibility to "good news the poor."

More than anyone else of our times, Mother Teresa exemplifies the best of Christian commitment as she and those of her order serve the poorest of the poor. Among people for whom all hope of a meaningful life is gone, she simply seeks to provide comfort and dignity during life's final hours.

A few years ago my wife, Pat, and I were invited to attend a reception hosted by Secretary of State and Mrs. James Baker for Mother Teresa at the Blair House across Pennsylvania Avenue from the White House. We were among a few representatives of the religious community included in a roomful of Washington's rich and famous. After her introduction she was presented with honors and gifts for her ministry to the poor.

Because of her frail health she spoke seated in a chair near the podium. A small woman with a soft voice, in broken English she thanked us for the generosity of the gifts and then told several stories of people who were serving with her in Calcutta. She talked about a U.S. senator who had spent several days making daily runs to serve the dying people. She praised a young couple about to be married who requested that, rather than wedding gifts, contributions be sent to the needy. In each instance she described how their lives had been enriched by reaching out to serve.

Had she described the destitution she knows as well as anyone, we would have been sympathetic, perhaps given more money, and returned to our homes and routines feeling better for having responded to her appeal. But that's not how the evening ended. She had spoken to our need to give as much as to the needs of the poor. We left quietly reflecting on the rewards of service as much as the demands upon our Christian conscience to respond to the poor and needy.

I think it was that way with the rich young man who Jesus instructed to sell his belongings as the first step toward discipleship. However wealthy he might have been, his personal fortune would have hardly made a dent in the poverty problem of his time. Jesus' instruction was meant as much for his own good as for the poor around him. Likewise when Zacchaeus offered to pay restitution fourfold to those he had abused, it was for his own salvation and well-being.

By any standard John Wesley earned enough money

through his published writings to be a wealthy man. While he was never destitute, he took a vow of poverty, giving away nearly everything he earned. This wasn't to earn his salvation, nor a means of persuading the urban poor of his day to faith in Christ, although that indeed happened. He lived this way as an expression of his understanding of the gospel. In the final analysis, compassionate ministry or compassion evangelism is neither a program or activity by which we try to earn God's favor nor a ploy or means to win people to our faith and build our churches. We live and share the gospel because it is the right thing to do. When we do the right thing, we can live with the confidence that good will result. Even if we don't see the results in our lifetime, we are assured of that ultimate approval, "Well done, good and faithful servant!" (Matt. 25:21, 23).

Appendix

Nazarene Compassionate Ministry Centers
April 1996

Appalachian Compassionate
Ministry Centers, Inc.
606-248-0409
730 Winchester Ave.
Middlesboro, KY 40965

Bethel Institute of Family
Services, Inc.
201-427-3255
681 High Mountain Rd.
North Haledon, NJ 07508

Bethlehem Ministries, Inc.
201-262-0534
P.O. Box 7225
Paterson, NJ 07510

Blue Hills Community Family
Life and Counseling Center,
Inc.
816-921-4557
5207 Wayne Ave.
Kansas City, MO 64110

Bresee Compassionate
Ministries, Inc.
415-751-3935
420 29th Ave.
San Francisco, CA 94121

Cambodian Christian
Community, Inc.
612-545-9622
1653 Blackstone Ave.
St. Louis Park, MN 55416

Cambridge Institute, Inc.
617-354-5065
234 Franklin St.
Cambridge, MA 02139

Care Ministry, Inc.
603-838-5941
33 Bishop's Cutoff
Lisbon, NH 03585

Carpenter's Connection, Inc.
606-581-0668
830 York St.
Newport, KY 41071

Center Street Mission, Inc.
702-348-2619
P.O. Box 968
Reno, NV 89504

Central Care Mission, Inc.
407-299-6146
4027 Lenox Blvd.
Orlando, FL 32811

Central City Community
Outreach, Inc.
213-689-1766
P.O. Box 13273
Los Angeles, CA 90013

Cherry Street Mission
Ministries, Inc.
419-242-5141
105 17th St.
Toledo, OH 43624

Children of the Shepherd, Inc.
213-953-8955
P.O. Box 906
Hollywood, CA 90078

Christian Companion
 Ministries, Inc.
916-568-1535
727 Bowles St.
Sacramento, CA 95815

Christian Counseling Services,
 Inc.
615-254-8341
P.O. Box 60383
515 Woodland
Nashville, TN 37206

Christian Social Concerns, Inc.
619-698-1560
P.O. Box 608010
San Diego, CA 92160

Columbia New Hope Ministries,
 Inc.
803-786-4334
P.O. Box 2386
Irmo, SC 29063-7386

Common Ground Ministries,
 Inc.
513-621-4673
2011 Mohawk Pl.
Cincinnati, OH 45214

Community Center of Personal
 Enrichment, Inc.
770-227-5035
1525 Zebulon Rd.
Griffin, GA 30223

Community Initiatives, Inc.
602-955-5850
5604 N. 24th St.
Phoenix, AZ 85016

Community of Hope, Inc.
202-232-9091
1417 Belmont St. N.W.
Washington, DC 20009

Compassionate Ministry Center,
 Inc.
216-394-5437
P.O. Box 4354
Warren, OH 44430

Cornerstone Ministries
 Association, Inc.
615-226-8593
P.O. Box 40249
Nashville, TN 37204

Cross of Christ, Inc.
616-627-5617
221 N. Bailey St.
Cheboygan, MI 49721

Crossroads of the Rockies, Inc.
303-922-8772
4201 W. Kentucky Ave.
Denver, CO 80219

Detroit Impact, Inc.
313-272-0004
9930 Greenfield
Detroit, MI 48227

Door of Hope Ministries, Inc.
813-821-1030
1225 9th Ave. N.
St. Petersburg, FL 33705

FAITH, Inc.
214-438-1881
P.O. Box 177662
Irving, TX 75017-7662

Foundation Dinners, Inc.
614-653-3233
1000 W. Fifth Ave.
Lancaster, OH 43130

The Foundation Stone, Inc.
508-563-2664
437 Boxberry Hill Rd.
Hatchville, MA 02536

Fountain of Hope, Inc.
614-258-6526
P.O. Box 06392
Columbus, OH 43206

Friendly Chapel FLAME, Inc.
501-371-0912
116 S. Pine
North Little Rock, AR 72114

Friends of the Homeless, Inc.
617-335-8429
8 Driftway
North Weymouth, MA 02191

Friends of the Lamb's, Inc.
212-575-0300
130 W. 44th St.
New York, NY 10036-4078

Friendship Community, Inc.
817-536-4581
P.O. Box 50816
Fort Worth, TX 76105

Frontline Ministries, Inc.
407-293-3000
P.O. Box 555445
Orlando, FL 32855

Golden Gate Community, Inc.
415-552-1700
1387 Oak St.
San Francisco, CA 94117-2116

Good Samaritan House, Inc.
209-891-0811
1927 Young St.
Selma, CA 93662

Good Shepherd Center, Inc.
412-588-2210
P.O. Box 422
Greenville, PA 16125

Greater Works Ministries, Inc.
301-449-4269
5205 Larwin Terr.
Camp Springs, MD 20748

Heritage Counseling, Inc.
905-451-7507
68 Rutherford Rd. N.
Brampton, ON L6V 2J1 CANADA

Home for New Beginnings, Inc.
864-292-3538
P.O. Box 8298
Greenville, SC 29604

Hope for Tomorrow, Inc.
804-276-5239
9107 Berry Patch Dr.
Chesterfield, VA 23832

Hope Ranch, Inc.
406-387-5003
P.O. Box 130428
Coram, MT 59913

Job Finders, Inc.
503-656-9407
16354 S.E. 135th Ave.
Clackamas, OR 97015-8929

Kansas City Rescue Mission, Inc.
816-421-7643
1520 Cherry St.
Kansas City, MO 64108

Life Centre Ministries, Inc.
902-865-1376
194 Churchill Downs Cir.
Sackville, NS B4E 2J6 CANADA

Life Line International, Inc.
918-747-2128
P.O. Box 702254
Tulsa, OK 74170

Living Hope Compassionate
    Ministries, Inc.
916-243-8066
1043 State St.
Redding, CA 96001

Los Angeles Mission, Inc.
213-629-1227
P.O. Box 5630
Los Angeles, CA 90055-0630

Love Link Ministries, Inc.
405-239-6219
P.O. Box 26262
Oklahoma City, OK 73126

Love Works Center for
    Compassionate Ministry, Inc.
619-221-2612
3900 Lomaland Dr.
San Diego, CA 92106

Lower Lights Ministries, Inc.
614-228-1262
1066 Bellows Ave.
Columbus, OH 43223

Memphis Leadership
    Foundation, Inc.
901-327-6670
3355 Poplar, Suite 308
Memphis, TN 38111

Mission Possible, Inc.
604-253-4469
543 Powell St.
Vancouver, BC V6A 1G8
    CANADA

Narrow Gate Ministries, Inc.
213-721-5558
P.O. Box 1813
Montebello, CA 90640

Nazarene Indian Bible College
505-877-0240
2315 Markham Rd. S.W.
Albuquerque, NM 87105

Neighborhood Christian Center,
    Inc.
901-452-6701
223 Scott St.
Memphis, TN 38112

Neighborhood Christian Center
    of Atlanta, Inc.
407-767-9833
2949 Laurel Ln.
East Point, GA 30344

Neighborhood Christian Center
    of Decatur, Inc.
205-351-7633
706 Bank St.
Decatur, AL 35601

Neighborhood Multi-Service
    Community Center, Inc.
1118 Foam Pl.
Far Rockaway, NY 11691

New Beginning Family Services,
    Inc.
510-522-1757
1415 Oak St.
Alameda, CA 94501

New Hope in the Rockies, Inc.
719-578-9523
829 S. Hancock Ave.
Colorado Springs, CO 80903

New Life for the World, Inc.
310-597-3301
524 E. Chapman
Orange, CA 92666-1677

New World Christian Ministries,
    Inc.
312-626-6577
5004 W. Chicago Ave.
Chicago, IL 60619

The Open Door, Inc.
617-479-3387
44 Broady Ave.
Quincy, MA 02169

Operation Care, Inc.
503-777-2264
5535 S.E. Rhone St.
Portland, OR 97206

P. F. Bresee Foundation, Inc.
213-387-2822
3401 W. Third St.
Los Angeles, CA 90020

Positive Alternatives, Inc.
313-971-5291
2934 Marshall St.
Ann Arbor, MI 48108

Quincy Crisis Center, Inc.
617-471-7075
P.O. Box 31
Wollaston, MA 02170

Reachout, Inc.
410-957-4310
P.O. Box 684
Pocomoke City, MD 21851

Rearguard Ministries, Inc.
205-661-7711
5028 W. Burma Rd.
Mobile, AL 36393

Restore Orlando, Inc.
407-246-0061
P.O. Box 568606
Orlando, FL 32860

Rising Son Ministry, Inc.
702-383-8282
1829 E. Charleston, Suite 100
Las Vegas, NV 89104

Samaan House, Inc.
410-947-3622
2033-35 Frederick Ave.
Baltimore, MD 21223

The Sharing Place, Inc.
416-762-3322
624 Annette St.
Toronto, ON M6S 2C4 CANADA

Shepherd Community, Inc.
317-636-3838
1625 E. Washington Blvd.
Indianapolis, IN 46201

Side by Side, Inc.
610-539-3333
P.O. Box 265
Fairview Village, PA 19409

Siloam Mission, Inc.
204-956-4344
707 Main St.
Winnipeg, MB R3B 1E5
    CANADA

Spring of the Spirit, Inc.
410-789-5253
4819 Indian Ln.
College Park, MD 20740

Sun Valley Indian Schools, Inc.
520-524-6211
P.O. Box 4013
Sun Valley, AZ 86029-4013

Sunset District Community
    Development, Inc.
415-665-0255
3016 Taraval St.
San Francisco, CA 94116

Total Health Education, Inc.
517-484-7700
2627 N. East St.
Lansing, MI 48906

United Relief Association, Inc.
718-712-1567
241-18 145th Ave.
Rosedale, NY 11422

Upper Room Compassionate
    Ministries, Inc.
603-595-2039
78½ R. Main St.
Nashua, NH 03060

The Way Station, Inc.
216-482-5072
202 E. Park Ave.
Columbiana, OH 44408

Wisconsin Nazarene
    Compassionate Centers, Inc.
414-342-5959
2904 W. Wells
Milwaukee, WI 53208

NOTES

Part I

1. For a full description of the origins of Nazarene Compassionate Ministries, see L. Guy Nees, *Winds of Change: 1980-85, The Church in Transition* (Kansas City: Nazarene Publishing House, 1991). In 1991 the responsibility for directing Nazarene Compassionate Ministries was divided, with Nazarene Compassionate Ministries in the United States and Canada being within the Church Growth Division, and Nazarene Compassionate Ministries International remaining within the World Mission Division.

2. Donald Dayton claims quite accurately that "the Holiness Movement differs from Fundamentalism and Evangelicalism in that it is more oriented to ethics and spiritual life than to a defense of doctrinal orthodoxy" (Donald Dayton, "The Holiness Churches: A Significant Ethical Tradition," *Christian Century*, February 26, 1975, 197). The Holiness churches are, however, without question included within the conservative body of American Christianity generally known as Evangelicalism. Nazarene leaders, ministers, and laypeople alike reflect the views and social issues typical of Evangelicals. In 1984 the Church of the Nazarene joined the National Association of Evangelicals.

3. H. Richard Niebuhr, *The Social Sources of Denominations* (New York: H. Holt, 1929).

4. For a discussion of the internal denominational concerns and external social and political influences that resulted in a retreat from the social concerns of the early Nazarenes, see Thomas G. Nees, "The Holiness Social Ethic and Nazarene Urban Ministry" (D.Min. thesis, Wesley Theological Seminary, 1976).

5. Oscar Lewis, *La Vida: A Puerto Rican Family in the Culture of Poverty* (New York: Random House, 1966). See also Ken Auletta, *The Underclass* (New York: Vintage Books, 1983). Descriptions of entrenched poverty as a "culture of poverty" or, as in the more recent characterization, a "permanent underclass," are controversial and bear theological as well as sociological reflection. They communicate the notion that at some point certain characteristics of poverty begin to perpetuate themselves. Lewis and the early cultural anthropologists wanted to describe the depths of poverty and the futility of short-term expedient reforms. More recently, however, the idea has been taken up by those who advocate less intervention in the lives of poor people when, in their view, poverty becomes a lifestyle. The possibilities of personal and social transformation through spiritual renewal challenge any resignation to permanent intractable poverty. Some within the Christian community have seemed to resign themselves to perma-

nent poverty by quoting Jesus: "For you always have the poor with you" (Matt. 26:11, RSV).

6. Nicholas Lemann, in *The Great Migration: The Great Black Migration and How It Changed America* (New York: Knopf, 1991), describes the movement of Mississippi delta Blacks to Chicago during and following the Great Depression. He summarizes public policy in the Great Society and War on Poverty programs as the government's attempt to respond to entrenched urban poverty.

7. For a survey of evolving and changing attitudes of Evangelicals and Fundamentalists from the 1950s to mid-1970s see "An Analysis of Evangelical Social Concern," in Thomas G. Nees, "The Holiness Social Ethic and Nazarene Urban Ministry."

8. Mark O. Hatfield, *Conflict and Conscience* (Waco, Tex.: Word Books, 1971); Mark O. Hatfield, *Between a Rock and a Hard Place* (Waco, Tex.: Word Books, 1976).

9. The International Union of Gospel Missions: An Association of Rescue Missions (1045 Swift Ave., North Kansas City, MO 64116) produces the newsletter *Rescue* and provides conferences and training materials. On the Salvation Army, see Edward H. McKinley, *Marching to Glory: The History of the Salvation Army in the United States of America, 1880-1980* (San Francisco: Harper and Row, 1980).

10. Michael Harrington, *The Vast Majority: A Journey to the World's Poor* (New York: Simon and Schuster, 1976).

Chapter 1

1. For a discussion of these references, see Dianne Bergant, "Compassion in the Bible," in *Compassionate Ministry*, ed. Gary L. Sapp (Birmingham, Ala.: Religious Education Press, 1993), 9-35.

2. Anthony J. Headley, Joe Boone Abbott, and Gary L. Sapp, "Compassion in Religious Counseling," ibid., 123.

3. Marshall McLuhan, *The Medium Is the Message* (New York: Random House, 1967).

4. Jim Wallis, "Evangelism Without the Gospel," *Sojourners*, July 1976, 4-5.

5. Dianne Bergant, "Compassion in the Bible," 9-35.

Chapter 3

1. For a bibliography with references to books and articles about the development of Nazarene Compassionate Ministries, write to Nazarene Compassionate Ministries, 6401 The Paseo, Kansas City, MO 64131.

2. Harvey Cox stirred a national debate over his predictions of the demise of organized religion. In *The Secular City: Secularization and Urbanization in Theological Perspective* (New York: Macmillan, 1965), he celebrated the freedom that cities provide. In *Religion in the Secular City* (New York: Simon and Schuster, 1984), he sought to correct these

earlier predictions, describing new expressions of spiritual vitality among Evangelicals and theological conservatives in particular.

3. For a copy of the *Directory of Nazarene Compassionate Ministries: United States and Canada*, contact the Nazarene Publishing House, P.O. Box 419527, Kansas City, MO 64141.

4. Gibson Winter, *The Suburban Captivity of the Churches: An Analysis of Protestant Responsibility in the Expanding Metropolis* (New York: Macmillan, 1962).

5. For an introduction to the "homogeneous unit" theory, that congregations that concentrate on one particular racial or ethnic group have the best opportunity for growth, see C. Peter Wagner, *Our Kind of People: The Ethical Dimensions of Church Growth in America* (Atlanta: John Knox Press, 1979).

6. For a full discussion of early Nazarene social ministry, see Thomas G. Nees, "The Social Concerns of the Church of the Nazarene During Its Formative Years (1895-1920) as Reflected in Its Official Publications," in "The Holiness Social Ethic and Nazarene Urban Ministry." A complete listing of these documents has been compiled by Stan Ingersol, denominational archivist for the Church of the Nazarene, in *To Rescue the Perishing, to Care for the Dying: Historical Sources and Documents on Compassionate Ministries Drawn from the Inventories of the Nazarene Archives*, Nazarene Archives, Kansas City, compiled in 1985.

Chapter 6

1. For a complete reading list, including these books, contact Nazarene Compassionate Ministries, 6401 The Paseo, Kansas City, MO 64131.